Blue Mountain Buckskin

A Working Manual

Dry-Scrape
Brain-Tan

by

Jim Riggs

Second Edition
Revised, Enlarged

Backcountry Publishing
Ashland OR
2017

Published by:
Backcountry Publishing
1700 East Nevada St
Ashland OR 97520
www.braintan.com

Printed on recycled paper in the United States of America.

10th printing October 2017
2nd Revised Edition

Library of Congress Cataloging-in-Publication Data

Riggs, Jim, 1945-2017
        Blue mountain buckskin : a working manual,
        dry-scrape brain-tan / Jim Riggs. - 2nd ed., Rev., Enl.
        140 p. : ill.; 22 cm.
        ISBN 0-9658672-1-8 (softbound)
        LCCN: 81-122145

        1. Buckskin. 2. Tanning. 3. Leather work. I. Title.

        TS980.B82 R53 2003   675.23 19

Wholesale Purchases:
We offer substantial discounts on bulk sales to organizations,
schools, and businesses. For more information 888 443-3826.

For Slim and Sonny, who
started it all, and for
all the Buckskin People,
past, present and future.

CONTENTS

Numerous drawings and photographs further illus-
trating the topics described in the text will be found
throughout the book within the sections they amplify.

ABOUT THIS BOOKLET...

This booklet began with my desire to share the methods I have successfully used to produce brain-tanned
buckskin. I believe that anyone with deer hides, in-
door or outdoor working areas, a few home-fashioned
tools, a little common sense and alot of old fashioned
hard work should be able to make and wear his own. The
purpose, then, of these scribblings is to stimulate
your interest and provide you with the information necessary for you to make your own buckskin by the best
methods that I currently know.

Written instructions are a poor substitute for
learning any skill firsthand, and the process of making
buckskin is no exception. Buckskin is best learned directly from someone accomplished in the procedure who
can show you, step by step, the sequential changes a
deer hide must undergo to become good buckskin.

Seek out older native Americans, old mountain men
(Yes, they do still exist--that's who introduced me to
buckskin) or the increasing number of younger people
living closely with the land, reviving old life supporting skills, who have already relearned the art of
making buckskin by the old methods. If your interest
is sincere, your heart in a good place and you are
willing to listen carefully and work hard, they will
show you what they know and you will learn more than
any instructional booklet can ever show you. It is
people, not books, that really teach you how to make
buckskin, but if you have not yet found the right people, this manual will at least get you started.

Methods used by other contemporary buckskin makers
will most likely differ in some respects from mine. I
know many people who make buckskin and no two use exactly the same tools or follow exactly the same procedures; some turn out beautiful buckskin and others need
a little more practice, but that is the way buckskin
is. Beginning with limited information is better than
not beginning at all; any buckskin is better than no
buckskin. Seek to improve your knowledge, continue to
refine your own methods and share what you learn.

The step by step instructions I describe here are
the procedures I currently use. Additional experience-
proved variations are also given. They are the results
of over ten years of experimentation, research and

"comparing notes" with others. Since I began, I have incorporated, deleted or changed many aspects of my process as my knowledge and understanding increased. I expect further changes are yet to come, for just as buckskin is the result of a process, learning to produce good buckskin is an ongoing process--cumulative knowledge put into practice. The procedures I describe here work well for me and I hope they are presented in a reasonably clear, logical and easy to follow sequence. Perhaps these instructions will save you some of the hassle of trying to produce buckskin from the many inadequate accounts that glut the literature.

I have not knowingly presented any false or misleading information here. My researches and experimentations have been broad and varied, but certainly not exhaustive. I have been collecting all the buckskin "recipes" I could dig up for years, and have found most of the numerous early written accounts of Indian tanning methods to be classic examples of the unintentional recording for posterity of inaccurate, incomplete or misleading information. Objective as they probably tried to be, the earlier students of anthropology, explorers and others were simply not sufficiently attuned linguistically, socially or culturally to native cultures to accurately observe, interpret and record an involved process as making buckskin. What they saw and recorded as fact was not always what was really happening, and they seldom were exposed to the entire process, step by step, start to finish. Some accounts and portions of others are descriptively accurate, but not detailed enough for the would-be modern tanner to implement. For example, an old account may state "The hide is then pulled until dry and soft." It neglects to mention that this may be an extremely arduous, conscientious, several hour process involving many variables. Many small but important techniques and subjective evaluations integral to producing good buckskin do not readily lend themselves to the notice of an alien observer nor to conveyance via the written word.

Unfortunately, most modern (twentieth century) "how-to" woodcraft, Indian craft, survival and tanning guides pass along the same misinformation, making it difficult for the novice tanner to get a solid, knowledgeable start; or worse, they leave him confused somewhere in mid-process when he encounters a problem not mentioned in the instructions. Once you have found a method that works and you have produced some buckskin, however, the older original accounts make interesting reading and you can pick up some useful information and procedures to try.

2

Adding to the confusion and discrepancies in the older tanning accounts are the geographical and cultural differences between aboriginal native groups. Nearly all native peoples that I have researched made some buckskin, but the importance of buckskin for clothing, the quantity made and to a great extent the quality varied considerably from group to group, region to region. It is only logical, for example, that people living in a humid southern environment would have different needs and would use different techniques than dwellers of the northern Rockies or the arid desert west. In each area a deer skin underwent the same basic steps (fleshing, dehairing, degraining, braining, softening, sometimes smoking, etc.), but the ways and means for accomplishing these steps differed tremendously. Modern buckskin makers will also have to develop procedures best suited to their own climates.

My researches into native tanning methods (written and personal sources) and comparisons of my methods with the sometimes drastically different but equally successful methods used by other contemporaries have convinced me that there is no single "right" way to produce buckskin. The proof is in the product, not the process, but a good product can only result from a workable process. I believe, then, that the key to producing good buckskin is in learning, through experience and study, the sequential changes a deer skin must undergo to end up as buckskin. One must learn to "read" the characteristics and progress of each skin during each step, and act accordingly. Once you understand what must happen to the skin in each step you can improvise all sorts of variations to suit your own unique circumstances and resources, as long as they do the job.

The dry-scrape process I use and describe here is similar to that used by several native groups, especially the northern Ojibwa of Manitoba (as recorded in literature), but identical with none that I know of. Mine could be called an eclectic process, as through experimentation I have incorporated whatever means worked best.

If you have never tanned before, I would suggest you read this booklet entirely through first. Then, on your first hide stick pretty closely to the steps and order described here. Once you have "the feel" for it--know just what the skin should do or be like at each stage--you can try varying methods.

I would be very interested to hear from any of you who follow the procedures I have outlined in this booklet or who develop equally workable personal variations. If you can't produce what you consider to be good buckskin from these guidelines, then it is time for me to do some rewriting! Happy and successful buckskinning.

In this second edition I thank Dick Jamison for use of the staking photo inside the front cover and fellow tanner Cary Groner for his drawings concerning the lighter side of making buckskin. Additional photos were taken by Stephen Anderson, Sheree Kahle and Caryn Talbot. Many other friends and students in my Malheur and Wallowa Mountain field station courses over the years have contributed to the information contained herein. I especially thank Sheree Kahle for proofreading the manuscript, making suggestions and corrections (By golly, "carcass" does end in double "s") and assisting with the final layout.

Jim Riggs
May, 1979
Buck Gulch, Middle Fork of the
John Day River, Blue Mountains

&

May, 1980
Lostine, Wallowa Valley
Oregon Territory

4

WHY BUCKSKIN ?

"If a body has to wear clothes at all,
buckskin is the only thing to wear next
to your own skin."   --Slim, 1969

In a "wear it 'til it falls off your back" contest,
well-tanned and well-made buckskin clothing will out-
wear and out-last any available commercial fabric that
I know of. My good friend and early teacher, the late
A. C. "Buckskin Slim" Schaefer, wore his "everyday"
buckskin shirt almost every day and almost until the
day he visited the other side and decided to stay
there--over forty years of wear and the shirt always
looked as if he might have made it just the week before! My own first shirt, I must admit, is not doing
that well. During its seventh year I had to begin put-
ting patches on it, but it is made from the very first
skins I ever tanned so I'm not complaining; patches or
not, I intend to keep it for the rest of my life.
Buckskin has been made and worn for thousands of
years by native Americans and, later, adopted as standard garb by the mountain men, traders and others who
moved into the wilderness. It could be argued that
they had little other choice of materials, but the ap-
plicability of buckskin for wilderness apparel cannot
seriously be questioned. It is strong, tough, durable,
soft, lightweight, versatile, warm and comfortable--
in short, functional. I can think of only one drawback and that may be due solely to my upbringing in a
society with pampered concepts of comfort: wearing
thoroughly soaked buckskin is a unique experience!
While not as warm as wet wool, wet buckskin is much
warmer than cotton and is akin to being inside a di-
ver's wetsuit (with a pungent, built-in smokey aroma).
It takes some getting used to, but then, so does cavi-
ar!
There are also personal, ideological reasons for
making and wearing buckskin. It comes from our bro-
ther creatures the deer. It keeps us in direct contact
with real and natural wilderness values wherever we may
be. With great appreciation and respect for the deer
for providing us with the raw material, the wearing of

buckskin clothing produced through our own intelligence, skill and hard work is a source of wellbeing and independence from rampant commercialism--perhaps a new beginning or a continuation of a sane concept of man in nature.

Two million deer are killed, mostly irreverently, by hunters in the United States of America each year. Hundreds of thousands more die on the highways. For most hunters the hide is a waste product sloppily slashed from the carcas and discarded. But what is waste due to the ignorance of one man can be clothing for life for another.

If brain-tanned buckskin were not appreciably better than commercially produced, chemically tanned deer hides, it likely would not be worth the dedication and effort required to make it, but real buckskin makes the chemical leathers seem like a waste of good hides. After making, seeing, feeling, smelling and wearing your own brain-tanned buckskin, your criteria and sense of values become irreversibly biased!

If you are looking for a quick and easy way to make good buckskin, forget it; this booklet is not for you. If you are willing to take some time, learn some new skills, commit yourself to those bloody, dripping, fat and flesh-covered deer hides bundled in plastic garbage bags that a friend left on your porch, read on.

Anyone you see wearing his own hand-tanned and handmade buckskin clothing has paid his dues, proven his sincerity and probably knows more than what shows. Pick his brain!

While I use the term "tanning" frequently in referring to the buckskin process, I do not consider buckskin to be tanned in the same context as commercial, chemically tanned skins. More properly, buckskin is manipulated and conditioned, but the skin structure is not chemically altered. Also, technically, deer have skins, larger animals (moose, elk, bison, etc.) have hides, but I use the two interchangeably (so you won't get bored from the repetition!).

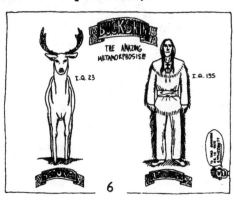

BUCKSKIN
THE AMAZING METAMORPHOSIS!!!

I.Q. 23   I.Q. 135

OBTAINING DEER HIDES

You don't have to hunt your own deer to obtain
hides. You may have to become quite a scrounger and
opportunist, but it will be worth it. I'd suggest collecting several hides if you can so that, if this is to
be your first attempt at making buckskin, all your ex-
pectations won't be riding with one hide. I find it
most efficient to run three or four skins through the
process together.

The best time to start looking for hides is just
before hunting season begins. Put feelers out all over
the area where you live; ask friends and friends of
friends who hunt to save their hides for you. Check
with custom meat processors, local stores that do their
own butchering, any place you can think of that might
receive deer hides. During hunting season take a drive
into the wild country--woods, mountains, national for-
ests--anywhere that hunters set up base camps. Stop by,
explain your purpose and see if they will give you
their hides. Alot of skins never make it out of these
hunting camps; many hunters just don't want to bother
with them and you can make good use of what otherwise
would be wasted.

Many farmers and ranchers living in lucrative deer
country have the populations all scoped out beforehand
and fill their tags the morning of opening day. The
fresh hides are tossed over a nearby fence or corral,
easy to spot and usually unwanted; stop and inquire.
Rummage through de facto roadside dumps (They're easy
to spot too, just look for signs declaring "DUMPING OF
RUBBISH PROHIBITED")! Also check regular garbage
dumps.

Road-kill deer are a good source of hides at any
time of the year but are in most areas, unfortunately,
illegal to possess. Sometimes you can explain your
needs to the state police or county sheriff and they
will "unofficially" let you retrieve the hides. Sometimes they will even keep you informed as to where
fresh road-kills are, especially if you agree to drag
the carcases off the road. (They may think you are a
little weird, but when they see you are sincere, they
will be helpful if they can).

If you can't obtain enough hides for free, you may
have to fork out a little money. Try placing want-ads
in your local newspaper, in the ubiquitous "Weekly Shop-

pers" or "Best Buys"--those ad-sheets commonly found at supermarket checkstands and laundromats. Many radio stations have community "buy, sell and trade" shows where you can place a request for free. Ask for un- wanted deer hides, offer to pay a couple bucks per hide, give a phone number where you can be reached and be willing to pick the hides up.

Most areas have commercial hide buyers who purchase as many hides as they can as cheaply as possible, then resell them to larger-scale, regional buyers or direct- ly to tanneries for a profit. Often they will sell to you as long as they still make their same profit. The disadvantage is that you will have to pay more, maybe upwards of three or four dollars per hide. The advan- tage is that you will have a large number of hides to sort through. Be extremely selective. To a certain extent, the larger the hide, the thicker the finished buckskin, so smaller skins are best for lightweight shirts, breechcloths, summer dresses, bags to be beaded or quilled, etc. Larger hides are best for winter shirts, coats, pants, vests, leggings, moccasins, robes, etc. A short, meaningful proverb should be stated here, however: "Don't count your buckskins before they are tanned!"

The main things to watch for when selecting hides are what I call scores or score-marks--knife cuts from improper skinning techniques slashed into the flesh sides of the skins. Light scores are okay, but reject skins with deep scores, ones that slice nearly all the way through. When a badly scored skin is stretched and dried in a frame, then scraped, these cuts will fre- quently split open. The neck and rump of a hide are us- ually scored the worst.

Bullet holes can also be a problem. Select hides with as few and small holes as you can find. A few holes around the edges are better than big "cannon holes" in the center of a hide. I cannot emphasize e- nough how many later, potential hassles you can avert by collecting well-skinned, unsliced hides. To parti- ally alleviate this problem, I collect as many hides for free as I can, look them over carefully and trade the heavily scored ones straight across, hide for hide to a local custom butcher for better ones. To him, one skin is as good as another as long as it is fresh and of comparable size because he is just selling them to a hide buyer anyway.

You may also be able to work out a barter system for securing hides. Several years ago a good friend approached a small-scale, one-man custom butchering out- fit specializing in the production of venison salami. The operator has a solid reputation for quality, and sometimes hundreds of local hunters bring their freshly-killed deer to him. My friend offered his time and expertise free of charge to skin all the incoming deer in exchange for the skins and brains. He did such a good job the first year that now he and/or close friends have a regular, paying job there each deer season and they make enough money to last them through the next year (they live primitively in the southwestern Oregon mountains and don't need much), plus, they have all the properly skinned hides their community can use. Each party benefits from the other's skills.

Thousands, maybe hundreds of thousands of deer hides are needlessly wasted each year. With these ideas, your own ingenuity and simply being in the right place at the right time, you too should be able to obtain all the deer hides you can use. Incidently, don't pass up opportunities for hides other than deer if they should arise. My own experience has been limited to deer and elk, but friends have successfully used goat and young calf hides for buckskin, and the literature also records pronghorn, bighorn sheep, moose and caribou. Domestic sheep skins seem to be too weak to withstand the vigorous buckskin process.

MOST BUCKS, WHILE ENDOWED WITH A CERTAIN AMOUNT OF COMMON SENSE, TEND TO BECOME SINGLE-MINDED DURING THE FALL RUT, AND, BY IGNORING CARS AND OTHER DEADLY OBJECTS, PROVIDE THE NON-HUNTER WITH A SOURCE OF BUCKSKIN.

9

SKINNING YOUR OWN DEER

I don't know if it's that hunters these days don't know how to skin deer, have forgotten or dismissed the idea of applying skill and personal pride to any endeavor or just plain don't care, but fully ninety-five per cent of the hides I examine each fall are improperly skinned. It is as if the modern "American Way" is one of slashing off the skin sheerly for the thrill of wielding a newly-purchased, custom-made knife! As far as I am concerned, there is only one way to skin a deer, and that is the right way. I'm sure others have their own "right ways," but here is mine.

A skin is more efficiently and nearly as expediently removed by "fisting" or "pelting" it off. This means separating the skin from the carcass using only your fingers and hands and eliminates the possibility of unnecessary and undesirable knife cuts in the skin.

Suspend the deer by a rope, one end tied around its neck right behind the ears, the other affixed over a tree limb, tripod of poles or any similar arrangement that allows you to hoist it off the ground. With a sharp knife, slit the skin from anus, up the center of the belly, chest and neck to the throat. Don't stab down through the skin into the carcass; to begin this cut, grab a pinch of skin between the hind legs, lift it away from the body and make a small cut through part of it. Then insert the tip of your knife into the cut between the skin and body and with the cutting edge up (facing you), slide the knife along, gently lifting it to cut, then sliding it under more skin, lifting to cut again, etc. Hold the knife with your index finger under the back of the blade for better control so you don't cut downward into the body cavity. Skinning should be a clean, bloodless job. A pocket knife or small, sharply-pointed sheath knife works better than a large skinning knife (in fact, I would only use a regular skinning knife if I had nothing else). If you prefer, you can begin this ventral cut at the sternum and work in both directions, or at the neck and work down, but always avoid cutting into the body cavity.

If the deer has already been field-dressed before skinning, this ventral cut will of course already run from anus to sternum (beginning of the ribcage), so just extend it up the chest and neck. Girdle the neck

skin just below the rope,
right behind the ears.
Cut only the skin, not into the neck meat, just as
you made the ventral cut.
If you want the tail skin
left on the hide, contin-
ue the ventral cut from
anus to tip of tail.

Next, make a slit
from the hooves (most
people prefer to begin
this cut at the next
joint up the leg, the
"knee," but I like to get
the entire leg skin with
the hide) all the way up
the inside-center of each
leg so that it connects
with the throat-to-anus
cut. Girdle the skin a-
round the legs wherever
you began this cut.

If it seems easier,
you can make all these
cuts while the deer is
still on the ground, then
hoist it up. If you have
no way to hang the deer,
this skinning method still
works fine on the ground,
but makes keeping the meat
and hide clean more difficult. With some experi-
ence, you can decide which
you prefer. Either posi-
tion is easier with a second person to hold the
deer's legs out of the way
while you make the cuts.

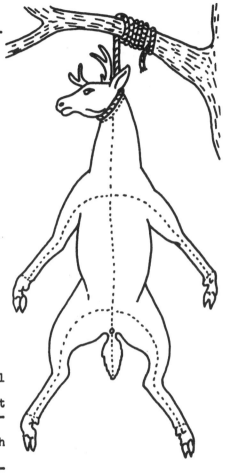

With the cutting completed, start at the back of
the neck and carefully and cleanly separate the skin
from the carcass. A small knife helps to get this
started. Make sure you are peeling back only the skin
and not any meat. You should see only whitish connective tissue between the loosened skin and carcass, no o-
pen red meat. Pull the skin away from the neck with
one hand and dig in with fingers and knuckles of the
other to separate the skin from the neck. I emphasize,
work carefully at first to make certain you are peeling
only skin. Pulling and separating, work your fingers

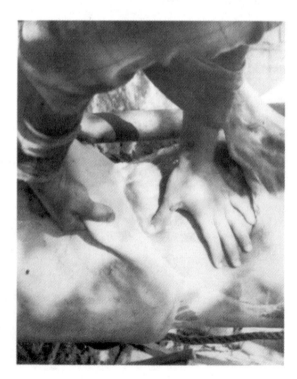

Fisting or pelting the skin from a deer suspended by it's neck. After making the initial incisions, a knife is not used.

Cleanly peeling the skin from a deer lying on the ground.

around to the throat slit and the skin should peel
cleanly. It is more difficult, especially for beginners, to get a clean start if you initially try to peel
the freshly-cut edges back from the throat slit. From
this point on, you should have little or no further
need for a knife.

If you are trying this skinning method for the
first time, work slowly until you get the feel of it.
Once you do, I believe you'll agree it is the most sen-
sible, natural way to keep both meat and hide unblemished. Continue peeling and separating the skin down
the neck, shoulders, front legs and back. Don't be a-
fraid to pull hard. Often the skin can be peeled
cleanly down the entire back with one concerted pull,
but again watch for meat that may want to adhere to the
hide. The large, thin sheets of flank meat (along ribs
and belly from pit to groin) are likely to give you the
most trouble. For best results, as on the neck, first
peel the skin further down on the back than on the
sides, then work your hands between skin and meat to-
wards the belly cut. In this way, the layers of flank
meat will stay on the carcass where they belong. Many
skins I have acquired from others had the entire flanks,
maybe five or six pounds of meat, left on the skin--
what a nonsensical waste!

Continue peeling down the rear legs and around the
rump (some lumps of fat often want to stick to the skin
here) until the skin is free of the carcass. Congratu-
lations! You have just mastered a long-forgotten skill.
A skin peeled from the carcass by this method (or other
workable variations) will be clean and will save you
time and work later because it will require no additional fleshing. Some connective tissue will remain on the
skin and will dry to a tough, thin, translucent sheet
which I call the membrane. For the skin to stretch,
soften and "fluff" into finished buckskin, this membrane must be broken up or entirely removed, but that
step will come later in the process.

You now have a clean skin, free of knife cuts,
flesh and fat and ready for the buckskin process. You
also have an intact deer carcass to provide you suste-
nance and strength while you work on the skin! Gutting
and butchering, not covered herein, are adequately described in many books and pamphlets, but if possible,
learn these important skills firsthand from someone experienced.

Should you encounter folks with unskinned deer when
you are out looking for hides, offer to do the skinning
for them by this method--and show them how as you work.
Obtaining good hides is well worth the effort you put
into it. Beginning the buckskin process with a badly-

scored deer hide is akin to starting an extended automobile trip with a bald tire--it will only get worse!

Some people prefer to hang a deer by the hind legs
for skinning. You can still fist a hide off this way,
but to me, it is backwards and more difficult to accomplish cleanly. When a deer is hung by the neck, or
if the deer is on the ground skinning is at least begun from the neck, peeling the skin is more like taking off the deer's coat; try to do it upside down and
everything else wants to come off with it!

Like many aspects of making buckskin, the skinning
procedure is easier to do in real life than to describe.
I hope you will find the opportunity to try this method
and I hope that my directions have not left you strand-
ed somewhere scratching your head in wonder.

fig. 1 : THE NATURE OF DEER

HERE, KITTY KITTY KITTY...

① EXHAUSTIVE BASIC RESEARCH HAS NOW PROVEN BEYOND REASONABLE DOUBT
THE UNWILLINGNESS OF MOST DEER TO BE SKINNED...

CARING FOR HIDES

If at all possible, obtain fresh, unsalted hides--
they are the easiest and cleanest to work with. If you
are in a situation where you must use salt (or else
lose the hide to spoilage), a pound or so sprinkled li-
berally over the flesh side, especially where meat and
fat are most evident, will help to draw out and drain
moisture, dry up the adhering flesh and fatty tissue
and preserve it for awhile, but a hide is best entirely
cleaned while fresh and allowed to dry naturally. Also,
I believe that salt, if not thoroughly washed from a
hide before it is stretched and dried in a frame, will
make the hide more brittle for the scraping process.
This is only my own opinion based on my own experience.
Unless you get fresh hides as soon as they are brought
in, most hides obtained from hide buyers will already
be salted for temporary storage, so you will have no
choice. Take what you can get; just remember to soak
and rinse salted hides well in water before taking them
through the buckskin process.

Most hides you acquire will have hunks and/or slabs
of meat and fat adhering to them. Whether you plan to
dry and store them or begin tanning right away, you
will have to flesh them first. Already-dried hides,
salted or unsalted, that were dried with meat and fat
on them, must be soaked in water until they are again
fully soft before they can be fleshed.

If the weather is cold (refrigerator temperature or
colder), you can store unfleshed hides for up to several weeks without dammage from deterioration occurring;
the sooner you can flesh them, the better, however.
Sealed in plastic bags and frozen, unfleshed hides will
remain good for at least a year. If unfleshed hides
are allowed to sit in the sun or remain generally warm
for even a few days, you run the risk of them beginning
to decompose or becoming "grease-burnt" (not to mention
them becoming very smelly!). The term "grease-burnt"
refers to heat-melted globs of fat soaking into the
skin. While not often evident at the time, the fatty
oils can weaken skin structure so that during the later,
vigorous softening process, the skin simply may not
hold together. It is surprising, though, what a raw or
green skin (as untreated hides are called) can undergo
and still turn into good buckskin. I have frequently
built up my fortitude, plugged my nose and cleaned up

some awfully rank skins covered with rotting flesh, rancid fat, dripping with deteriorating blood and other
bodily fluids and seething with maggots--I just didn't
want to see them go to waste!

When I collect a great number of hides during hunting season, I cannot carry them all through the buckskin process as fast as I get them, so my main priority
is to get them all fleshed, then dried for convenient
storage. If time does not permit fleshing all of them
either, and if some of the skins are already dried and
not too obnoxiously covered with fat and flesh, I'll
take a chance and store them "as is" for awhile, but
soak up, flesh and use those hides first when I begin
the tanning process. Fat is worse than dried meat when
left on a hide; the risk of spoilage is reduced if you
at least peel off the larger hunks.

The easiest way to dry hides is to simply spread
them out, flesh side up, on dry ground, hang them from a
clothesline or just drape them over poles, hides frames,
fences, woodpiles, etc. But dried in these ways they
will shrink up, become stiff and unwieldy and require
more storage space when dry. You also must make certain that the edges do not curl and remain moist while
the greater expanse of the hide is drying. Flies will
sometimes lay eggs in these protected crannies and
there is more chance of spoilage from heat and moisture.
A little fine sawdust or dry dirt rubbed into the edges
will help to promote speedier drying and prevent curl-
ing. Clothespins or small sticks may also be used to
prop the edges open. If you don't heed this warning,
you may find that the slits you cut around the edges of
a hide to tie it into a frame will rip out more easily.

Hides will dry more quickly if lightly stretched
and tacked, again flesh side out, to barn or shed walls.
If you have extra frames built, you can tie some of the
skins in those to dry and leave them there in preparation for scraping. Hides stretched and dried will be
thinner and can be easily rolled up, several together,
for space-saving storage. All dried hides should be
stored in dry places. They are best sealed in large
plastic trash bags, rolled up tightly in a large sheet
of plastic or other tarp with the ends tied closed or
placed in a sealable container safe from clothes moths,
carrion beetles, mice, mildew, etc. Well-fleshed,
dried hides, properly stored, will remain good for
years. If drying is not feasible where you live, roll
up the freshly-fleshed hides, seal them in plastic bags
and freeze them until needed.

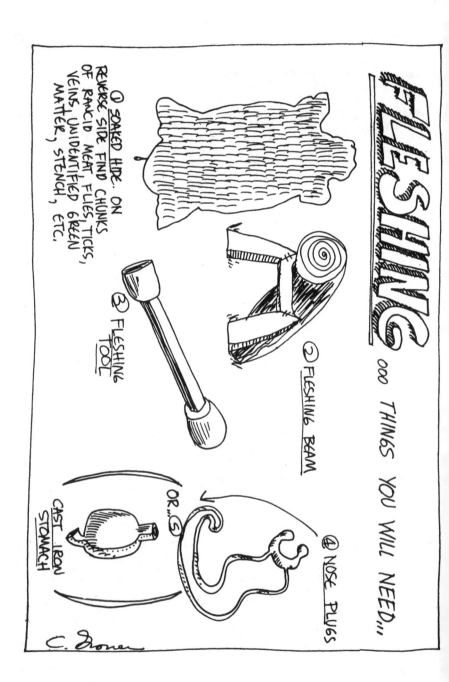

FLESHING

ooo THINGS YOU WILL NEED...

① SOAKED HIDE. ON REVERSE SIDE FIND CHUNKS OF RANCID MEAT, FLIES, TICKS, VEINS, UNIDENTIFIED GREEN MATTER, STENCH, ETC.

② FLESHING BEAM

③ FLESHING TOOL

④ NOSE PLUGS

OR...S

CAST IRON STOMACH

C. Grouse

18

FLESHING TOOLS AND PROCEDURES

Fleshing is the process of cleaning all meat and fat from a hide and is best done as soon as possible unless a hide is to be stored as previously described. Fleshing is a necessary, preparatory step to the rest of the buckskin process unless you are dealing with already-cleaned hides. There are several ways to accomplish fleshing; here are a few.

If you have only one or two hides and plenty of time, or if the hides are relatively clean already, you can do an adequate fleshing job with only your hands, a sharp rock or a knife. Just pull, peel, scrape or cut off all the meat and fat. As with skinning, take care not to cut into the hide. Bits of connective tissue (or anything else small that doesn't look like meat or fat and doesn't want to come off) can be left on the skin for now. Remember, a dry or partially dry hide should be soaked in water long enough to loosen any meat or fat as requisite to fleshing.

Fleshing is more easily, quickly and efficiently accomplished with some simple but more specialized tools (see illustrations). I prefer to drape the skin over a five or six foot long, six to twelve inch diameter log beam with a smoothed, slightly flattened one to two foot long surface at the upper end. The beams I prefer are of aged cottonwood because it seldom cracks or splits and the working surface remains fairly smooth. Poplar, aspen or large willow logs are probably as good as cottonwood. Choose dead wood for your beam; freshly-cut and peeled green wood will often crack as it dries. I have also used sections of pine and fir logs. They work fine for fleshing skins with the hair still on, but through concerted use and repeated wetting and drying tend to continually crack and splinter, making the working surface rough and uneven. This makes them less satisfactory for the membraning step, later in the process, in which the hair has already been scraped from the skin and no longer can cushion it. Any rounded log will probably work, especially if it is all you have; just be sure to keep the working surface well-smoothed so it won't wear unwanted holes in your hides. In a pinch, any roundish, smooth surfaces can suffice (oil drums, pontoons, canoe bottoms, car fenders, etc.). Where there is a will and available resources, there is a way!

If you have a permanent place to work and plan to do
several skins, you might as well make a good, dependa-
ble, functional beam. I believe wood is much better
than makeshift metal surfaces because it has some
"give" and you are less apt to scrape holes in a skin
while fleshing. A log beam is portable and is commonly
used in either of two positions. It can be leaned nearly upright against a wall or tree with the skin draped
over the top of it. The skin is held in place between
the top of the beam and the surface against which the
beam leans. As fleshing proceeds, the skin is readjust-
ed. The fleshing motion is a downward pull, toward you,
with your fleshing tool. The log beam can also be propped in a much more slanted position on legs or other
supports with the working end at waist level and the
butt end resting on the ground. With the waist beam the
skin is draped over the working end and is held in place
with one thigh pressed against it while you work. The
fleshing motion is a downward push, away from you. I
recommend either of these beam arrangements, whichever
is most comfortable for you. I prefer the waist beam,
but occasionally switch just for the variety and change
of muscles used. You can make a beam as elaborate and
finished as you desire, but all that is really necessary
is that it be sturdy and have a smoothed working surface
at the upper end.

Fleshing was undoubtedly one of the functions of the
multipurpose chipped stone scrapers so common at old Indian campsites. Other more specialized stone and bone
fleshing tools were also used aboriginally. The canon
bone (the long-bone nearest the hoof in the lower front
legs of deer, elk, moose, etc.) was one of the most common. The cleaned bone is cut in two on a bevel at the
lower end, just above the joint, and tiny, sharp teeth
are filed into the chisel-shaped end. A buckskin loop
is tied or run through a hole drilled at the top of the
bone for a wrist brace (as on a skipole grip). This
flesher is used in a stabbing, scraping motion to peel
fat and flesh from a hide draped over the upright beam,
stretched and pegged to the ground or sometimes fresh-
ly-laced into a frame. I have made and used these canon bone fleshers and they work (the larger elk or moose
bones are best), but have found a metal bar to be faster
and more efficient.

The standard fleshing tool I use and prefer is a
sixteen inch length of old automobile leaf spring one
and a half inches wide and a quarter inch thick. These
dimensions were not planned, I just scrounged around
junkpiles until I found a piece that seemed about right.
Longer sections of leaf springs or other metal bars can

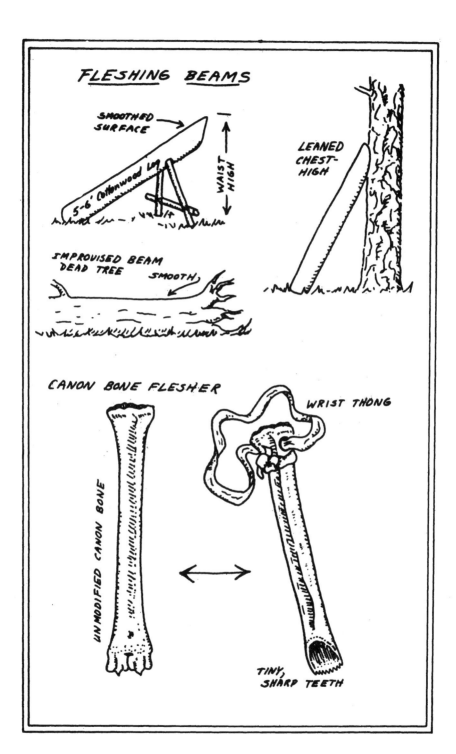

FLESHING BEAMS

SMOOTHED SURFACE

5-6' Cottonwood Log

WAIST HIGH

LEANED CHEST-HIGH

IMPROVISED BEAM DEAD TREE

SMOOTH

CANON BONE FLESHER

UNMODIFIED CANON BONE

WRIST THONG

TINY, SHARP TEETH

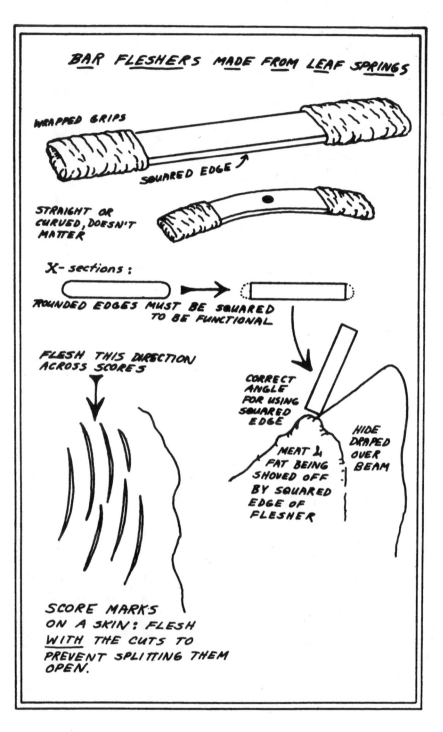

BAR FLESHERS MADE FROM LEAF SPRINGS

WRAPPED GRIPS

SQUARED EDGE

STRAIGHT OR CURVED, DOESN'T MATTER

X- sections :

ROUNDED EDGES MUST BE SQUARED TO BE FUNCTIONAL

FLESH THIS DIRECTION ACROSS SCORES

CORRECT ANGLE FOR USING SQUARED EDGE

HIDE DRAPED OVER BEAM

MEAT & FAT BEING SHOVED OFF BY SQUARED EDGE OF FLESHER

SCORE MARKS ON A SKIN: FLESH WITH THE CUTS TO PREVENT SPLITTING THEM OPEN.

be cut to more convenient length with a cutting torch, grinding wheel (girdled deeply, then snapped in two) or hacksaw (good exercise!). Whole and broken sections of leaf springs are surprisingly common just lying around old farms, homesteads, junkyards, etc., and can be extremely useful to the penniless but enterprising buckskin maker (see section on making hide scraper blades).

My favorite leaf spring flesher has a slight bow to it (natural curve of the spring) but straight ones are equally functional. Leaf springs usually have either squared or rounded edges. Already-squared edges need only to be honed-up to accentuate the squareness (the working part of the flesher). Mine were rounded and thus needed further modification. First with a grinding wheel and later with hand files I ground away the rounded edge until it was flat, perpendicular to the one and a half inch width, and had pronounced, squared corners (see illustrations if you are a bit confused). About four inches of each end is wrapped and bound with cloth to form comfortable grips, as the tool is held in both hands.

To flesh a hide on the waist beam, the fleshing bar is held horizontally, but tilted back slightly so that only one squared edge is pushed along the hide. With forward and downward pressure, the squared edge gets a good bite and efficiently separates the flesh and fat from the skin. Used in this manner, the bar fleshing tool will not damage the hide, even when strong pressure is applied to remove stubborn hunks or slabs of meat. Care must be exercised, however, not to let the bar slide sideways, as even the squared edge can slice into the skin with that motion. When fleshing, I drape the skin over the beam and usually begin near the center, working toward the edges until the skin is clean. Wherever you begin, large sheets of meat can usually be shoved off in their entirety. The bar flesher works equally well on the upright beam, but the grip and angle are adjusted for a pulling motion.

Anytime a hide is soaked in water for a couple days or more, the hair often begins to "slip," to fall off the skin. Since the hair must otherwise be scraped off anyway later in the process, I often turn the hide over on the beam and with the flesher shove off all the hair that wants to come. This maneuver is standard procedure in the wet-scrape buckskin process, only the hide is usually soaked long enough so that the grain or epidermal layer of skin can be shoved off at the same time. Dehaired hides will dry faster when laced into the frames, but dehairing a hide during the fleshing step is not integral to the dry-scrape method for making buckskin--it's just handy when it happens.

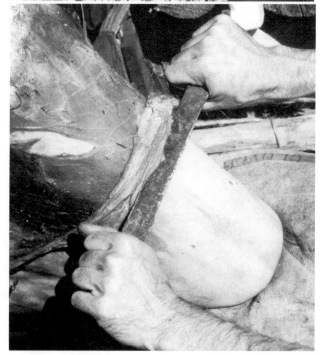

Fleshing on the waist beam with the square-edged metal bar flesher.

All that meat should have been left on the carcass, not the hide!

24

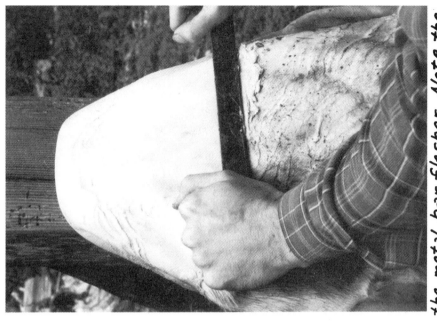

Fleshing on the upright beam with the metal bar flesher. Note the profusion of score marks on the skin.

25

Whenever you are handling hides that have been soaking for some time, be extremely careful if you should have any open cuts on your hands; without a thorough washing and disinfecting afterwards, there is a strong possibility of infection occurring. I know!...so be careful.

Leaf springs are not mandatory for making fleshers; they are just something I came across that works well. The cutting ridges can be ground from the edges of large old files, the back edge of a single-bladed drawknife can be ground square, discarded or broken parts from old farm machinery can be used (often with no modification necessary). In fact, any flat metal bar can be used providing the edges are squared and it is long enough to grip comfortably and still give you a six inch or longer working edge. If you don't have a handy junkyard to sort through, I suppose you could purchase a suitable bar from a steel company or machine shop. I prefer to scrounge about for the materials I need for tools and modify them myself (if practical) to suit my own needs. It is more satisfying, more fun and much cheaper!

Commercially manufactured fleshing tools of varying styles (mostly similar to drawknives) are available from tanning and taxidermy supply houses, but are expensive. I would not recommend that a novice tanner begin fleshing his first deer hide with a sharp blade unless he intends to produce a buckskin fishnet! Likewise, in the wet-scrape buckskin process it has been my experience that a sharp drawknife is often necessary to remove the stubborn grain from a wet hide draped over the beam; even with practice I find this a delicate and trying operation.

When you are fleshing a hide with the bar flesher, be especially careful around any scored areas. Flesh over them in the same direction they run, not across (perpendicular to) them, or you may deepen them or cut all the way through the hide. On the first hides I ever fleshed on a beam, I was not aware of some badly-scored areas (I didn't even know what a score was then!). I worked diligently to clean off those strange rows of stubborn tissue, only to realize later that I had been trying to remove the scored skin itself, and in so doing, had worsened the cuts (and they are still there, inside my first shirt!).

If fleshing becomes too dificult because the skin begins to dry out too much, remoisten the area with water. If still too tough, resoak the whole hide until it is thoroughly saturated and try again. Sometimes very dry meat (essentially jerky left on the hide) may take several days to soak up. It has been my experience that some connective tissue, or membrane, remains on the skin even after thorough fleshing by this method. It will be removed later.

With a functional fleshing tool (there are many variations I have not described here--improvise!) and a good beam, I believe you will encounter no insurmountable problems. You could have fleshed four hides during the time it has taken me to write this step!

Another few words of warning are warranted at this point: Deer hides, deer hair, deer flesh, deer fat, deer brains, et al., attract esurient (better look that one up!) dogs. They will immerse their heads over a foot to reach soaking hides, drag away hides waiting to be fleshed, chew the legs off hides laced in frames, chew open plastic bags and knock over large, covered cans to get hides, steal hides left soaking in the brain emulsion in a ten gallon bucket, even when they had to chew through two inches of ice that had formed on the surface after a particularly cold night, ad infinitum! I am speaking from experience. I even lost my best old steel flesher to a dog who, I guess, just carted it away so he could lick off all the rancid deer fat at his leisure. So, during any stage of the buckskin process, NEVER LEAVE HIDES WHERE DOGS CAN GET TO THEM, even for a few minutes!!! Every buckskin maker I know has encountered "the dog problem." I sincerely hope I have made this warning perfectly clear, and that you don't personally have to learn this lesson the hard way.

Now, let's get back to business.

" RIPE "
FOR
FLESHING!

27

BUILDING HIDE FRAMES

Fleshing is the first important step (other than skinning) in the preparation of all skins destined for any type of tanning process. After fleshing, the necessary, specific steps for the dry-scrape buckskin process begin. The first of these is tying the skin into a frame to dry, and this of course requires you to construct one or more frames (see illustrations).

Functional frames can be constructed of many varied styles and materials. I prefer straight pine, fir or tamarack poles at least two or three inches in diameter and about seven or eight feet long (some are later trimmed), but almost any sturdy, straight poles or squared lumber will work. Three by threes are excellent if you can find any, four by fours are super-sturdy, two by fours (or anything smaller) are a bit lightweight unless strongly braced at the corners or paired and nailed together to make "pseudo four by fours."

Frames must be constructed sturdily. As a deer hide dries, it shrinks and puts great tension on the ties and frame. If a frame is made of flimsy poles or boards or the corners are not joined solidly, the drying skin will often twist, warp or loosen the frame. It is difficult to scrape a hide well in a frame that wobbles or is not square. Save yourself some trouble; build sturdy frames!

The large ends of old broken or warped tipi poles can be recycled into hide frames. When loggers or timber thinners leave an area you can find an abundance of suitable poles in the slash piles they leave behind, or you can cut your own from thickets that could use a little thinning. If you can't find any of the stronger, heavier woods, reasonably straight juniper, alder, aspen, cottonwood, even large willows will work, but are lighter-weight and not as satisfactory. All these work better if they are already dead, or peeled and allowed to dry, then made into frames. As is necessary with many primitive skills, make the best of the resources you have available.

The sizes you build your frames will depend largely on the sizes of the hides you intend to stretch in them. I have several frames of varying sizes to accommodate small deer skins up to large elk hides. A frame with inside dimensions of roughly four to four and a half feet wide by five and a half feet high should be adequate for

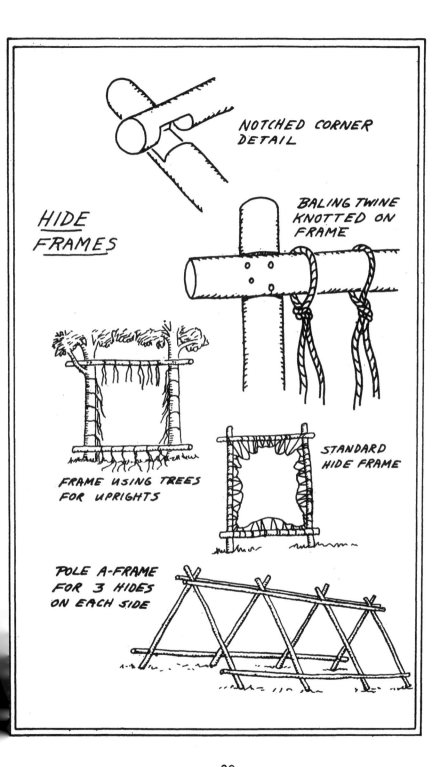

NOTCHED CORNER
DETAIL

HIDE
FRAMES

BALING TWINE
KNOTTED ON
FRAME

FRAME USING TREES
FOR UPRIGHTS

STANDARD
HIDE FRAME

POLE A-FRAME
FOR 3 HIDES
ON EACH SIDE

most average-sized deer hides. My frames for very large deer hides are five to five and a half feet wide and six and a half feet high. Remember to cut poles longer than the inside dimensions so the corners can overlap and so no matter which way it is turned, the frame stands on its own little legs. Sometimes while scraping, but especially while staking, it is convenient to turn the frame to one side or the other or even upside down to cover otherwise hard to reach areas of the hide. The legs raise the cross-poles a few inches off the ground and make tying or untying the ropes much easier.

An easy way to ascertain a proper frame size is to spread a wet hide out on the ground, lay your intended frame poles around it and assemble the poles to fit the hide. Of course, the next hide you do may be of a different size, so it is handy to have several frames of varying sizes. A hide should fit snugly in the frame--small hides in small frames and large hides in large frames. A small skin strung in the middle of a large frame tends to slacken, quaver and make steady scraping pressure and rhythm more erratic.

For sturdy corners I notch the poles (as in log cabin construction) a foot or so from each end with saw, chisel and hammer so they interlock together closely, then nail them in place. More simply, you can flatten the two surfaces to be meshed with an axe, then nail them together. If you have no nails, lash the corners, but make sure they are tight. I have also made sturdy frames by drilling the corners and pegging them together with hardwood (yew) pegs. A well-constructed frame should have no sway or wobble to it.

I prefer to build individual frames that can be easily moved (sun to shade, under cover if it rains, etc.). Should you have no convenient walls or trees to lean frames against, you can use a tripod of tipi poles for a brace, bind two single frames together at their tops in A-frame fashion, etc. Some friends who do alot of buckskin made a long, permanent A-frame structure of poles with spaces for four or five

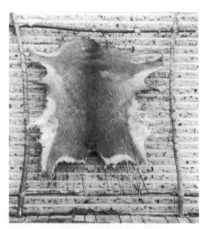

This frame is too flimsy. The drying hide has warped the skinny poles & has "wrinkled," which will make scraping more difficult.

hides on each side. You can also use two small, conveniently spaced trees for the sides of a frame and nail or bind cross-poles to them. Stationary frames are less satisfactory, however, because they can't be turned over or around. If you have no better options (as in a survival situation) you can peg a hide to flat, unrocky ground to dry, but this arrangement is seldom satisfactory, awkward for scraping because you are more apt to cut into the hide due to irregularities in the ground surface and not recommended (deer hides are not as thick as buffalo hides!).

STRINGING HIDES IN FRAMES

Stringing a hide in a frame requires an abundance of cordage. I use baling twine because it is free for the asking from nearly any farm or ranch that uses hay and because it is expendable (nothing lost if you must cut it, no hassle if it's left out in the weather, etc.). I prefer the natural fiber twine over the gross black, orange or blue and white peppermint-striped plastic stuff because knots do not slip as easily and, well, I just don't like plastic! But the plastic fiber is better than nothing if it is free. Any roughly quarter inch thick cord will suffice. I have come to prefer baling twine because it comes in exactly the right lengths (each piece about nine feet) for the method I use to tie a skin into a frame.

About every six or eight inches all the way around the frame I loop a length of twine at its midpoint around the pole and affix it with a simple overhand knot. This leaves the two four foot ends hanging from each tie point. Each of these ends will pass through one or two slits along the margin of the hide and tie it to the frame. Some people prefer to use several long ropes to bind the skin in the frame, running each around and around--through the hide, around the frame, through the hide again, etc. I think this method makes evenly positioning and stretching the hide more difficult, and should one or more slits in the skin rip out, the entire rope must often be retightened. Sometimes a combination of single and multiple ties works well--single ties position the hide at key points, then longer ropes are used inbetween. Other people use a series of metal hooks to hold a hide in a frame. There are many ways to tie a skin into a frame; I'm sure you will figure out methods that work well for you.

With all the ropes tied to the frame, you are ready to tie the skin in place. The skin must be soft and pliable, no dry or hard spots. A hide fresh from the deer, if cleanly skinned or if just-fleshed and still pliable, can be tied directly into the frame, but I prefer to soak any hide in water first (half a day for a fresh hide is sufficient). I think the water-soaking makes them stronger and less apt to rip from stress at the tie points. Previously dried hides must, of course, be re-soaked for a couple days (or until soft) prior to stretching.

Spread out the hide, flesh side up, on flat ground,

boards, old piece of carpet, etc. (to prevent dulling your knife tip). Stretch it out symmetrically to its full size and make sure no edges remain curled over or under. With a sharp, pointed knife cut one inch long slits about one third inch in from and parallel to the margin of the skin (whichever way the irregular edges may run) every three or four inches around the entire hide. This usually means cutting forty to sixty slits. If you cut the slits closer to the edge than about one third inch, there is more chance of them ripping out; if cut further in, you will be wasting some good potential buckskin. Later in the process, most of the outer edge of the skin will be trimmed off.

A water-soaked hide is ready to be laced into the frame.

Wet deer hides are tough, and you'd better use a sharp, straight blade for cutting the slits. Folding knives have a tendency to do just that--snap closed under pressure and slice your fingers. The reason for cutting one inch slits parallel to the edges is because they are stronger and provide more even tension as the hide dries. On the first hide I ever tanned, I thought I knew more than I really did (sometimes I still do!). With a leather punch I made little holes an inch apart real close to the edge thinking I would be saving more hide (this was contrary to Slim's instructions). When the skin dried in

32

Tying a water-soaked hide into the frame.

A very large mule deer hide, well-tied & dried in the frame.

the frame, nearly half of them ripped out and I had to untie, resoak, cut proper slits in from my ripped-out punch holes and restretch the skin in the frame, thus losing more hide than if I had done it the first time the way I had been taught!

The hide should be tied into the frame hair side out. Take notice of the shape of the hide as spread on the ground and maintain that properly proportioned shape as you tie it into the frame. I prefer to do the tying with the frame leaned upright, but if this seems awkward to you, make the first key ties with the frame on the ground, then stand it up.

Begin by tying each side of the top of the neck skin near the top-center of the frame. Run the twine through the slit, cinch it up snugly and wrap the remaining length several times around the pole. Finish by running the end under the taut twine that supports the weight of the hide and pulling it up tightly. This binds the free end of the twine against the pole under the tensioned twine. This may not seem like a complete knot, but the twine slipped under itself and cinched up tightly holds well and can be simply pulled loose when you go to remove the hide after scraping (untying fifty regular knots takes alot more time!). I believe that pole frames work better than lumber frames for these "friction" bindings. If these directions are not clear enough for you to follow, fasten the ties as you see fit--you'll soon come up with a workable system.

Next make a couple ties near, or directly to, the bottom corners of the frame, fastening them in the same manner as the neck. Now the skin should be well-centered and easy to keep symmetrical as you next tie the front legs, then all the rest until all slits are used. Make a tie on one side, then tie the corresponding spot at the other side to keep the skin stretched evenly. Strive for balance and even tension. Cinch each tie up to stretch the skin taut, but don't make it "drum" tight; it will shrink and further tighten as it dries. Be careful while tying the rump and tail area because the skin is weaker there and rips more easily. Sometimes I make no ties, or else don't pull them as tight there to prevent tearing.

As tying progresses, you may have to retighten a few of your earlier ties. It takes a little practice to string a hide in a frame well every time. When you have finished, the skin should not sag or be loose anywhere. Occasionally you will have to cut a few new slits and add some new ropes to take up slack. Press your fingers all around the circumference of the hide and anywhere an edge is not tight, make a new slit and tie.

Freshly-framed hides are best dried in the shade, or

only partial sun. A freshly-strung hide suddenly zapped by hot summer sun will dry too unevenly. The thinner areas of the skin will dry too fast, and when the rest dries and shrinks, these will "wrinkle" from the tension and be harder to scrape. In arid climates a hide will dry within a day. In humid regions or in cooler weather, it may take longer and be necessary to leave it in direct sun. You will probably have to do some trial and error experimenting to determine what works best in your area.

You can begin the scraping procedure as soon as the hide is nearly or completely dry. You will be able to determine when it is still too damp--your scraper blade will slip and slide and not get a good bite into the hair and grain. It is best to scrape a hide as soon as possible once it is dry. When a framed hide sits around for several days or more, it stretches and slackens with each day and night and eventually becomes looser in the frame.

TYING A HIDE IN THE FRAME

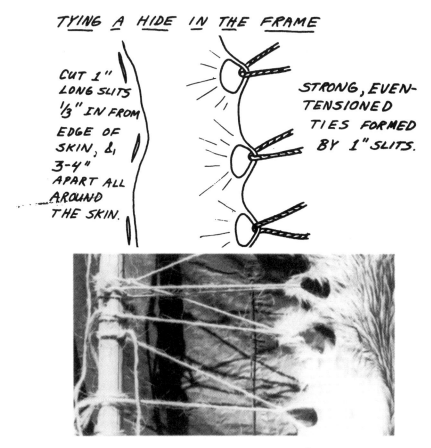

CUT 1" LONG SLITS 1/3" IN FROM EDGE OF SKIN, & 3-4" APART ALL AROUND THE SKIN.

STRONG, EVEN-TENSIONED TIES FORMED BY 1" SLITS.

MAKING A HIDE SCRAPER

A scraping tool of some sort is necessary for removing the hair and the grain from a skin by the dry-scrape method. Chipped or ground stone and bone scrapers, many of extremely fine workmanship, were made and used by native Americans before the introduction of steel, but steel was quickly adopted as soon as it became available. The hide scraper is the singly most important tool in the dry-scrape buckskin process. Besides scraping, it can serve as a fleshing tool and for helping to work the hide soft and dry during the staking process. To the best of my knowledge there is no such entity as a commercially manufactured hide scraper (although "trade blades" were once manufactured and distributed to various native groups by the Hudson's Bay Company and others) so you will have to make your own.

A hide scraper consists of two separate parts, the handle and the blade. I believe the blade is best tightly bound onto the handle with long buckskin laces (or other cord, since you haven't finished your own buckskin yet) rather than being permanently screwed or bolted in place. This way it can be easily and quickly removed when major resharpening or reshaping on a grinding wheel become necessary.

The easiest handles to find in nature are sections of tree limbs, either where they project out from the main trunk or further out where the branches fork. You will gain an interesting perspective on trees when you go out searching for your perfect scraper handle. When you find one that appears suitable, examine it from all angles before cutting--what looks right from one view may be absurdly misshapen from another. I believe it beneficial (and only fair) to explain to the tree why you are cutting into it and to thank it for providing you with an important tool.

Heavy, dense hardwoods make the best handles because a scraper works better if it has some weight to it. My best wooden handles are of yew, mountain mahogany and service berry. Madrone and oak are good, juniper and hawthorn okay, but lighter. Try to find a handle of the heaviest wood that grows in your region.

Cut a limb at least one and a half to two inches in diameter, one that gives you a firm, stable and comfortable grip. Remember, the limb will be smaller after the bark is peeled. Skinny handles tend to wobble and twist

during use and require a tighter (and more tiring) grip.
At the front end the handle should be wide enough, usually about one and a half inches, to accommodate the
blade. Some people prefer handles a couple feet long,
others shorter ones, around twelve to fourteen inches.
I started with longer handles but now prefer shorter
ones, providing they are heavy enough. You will learn
your preference through experience--whatever length feels
and works best.

Limbs can be simply cut from the tree in the desired
size (you might try a longer handle first, then shorten
it if desired). Limbs extending directly from the trunk
can be sawed first, then split out, in the same manner
the corners of your hide frames were notched. Peel the
bark, smooth any rough or sharp places (that might give
you blisters) and shape the head so the blade will lie
flush on it for secure binding. Keep in mind that green
wood is apt to split or crack as it dries; use dead wood
for handles if you can find suitably shaped pieces.

My first hundred hides were all scraped with wooden-
handled scrapers and I have no complaints, but I now believe the very best handles are fashioned from roughly
foot long sections of two inch plus diameter elk antler.
The antler is considerably heavier than any of the woods
and is a joy to use. Sometimes it seems to scrape the
hide all by itself! You can sometimes get two or three
handles from a single, large antler, although the diameter narrows at the tines. Like wooden handles, antler
will have to be cut to size, sometimes smoothed and
shaped to hold the blade. Elk antler handles, well-
formed and polished from use, were favorites of many native groups and were handed down from one generation of
tanners to the next. You can get some good ideas for
your own from specimens frequently on display at museums.

Good, sharp scraper blades are a must. I have found
flat (quarter inch or less thick) pieces of steel one to
two inches wide and long enough (about three to six inches) to be conveniently bound onto a handle to work
best. Coincidentally, sections of automobile·leaf
springs fulfill these requirements perfectly. The cutting edge of a scraper blade (as viewed from the top) is
rounded rather than straight. The rounded edge allows
you to apply pressure while scraping without corners cutting into the hide. End sections of many leaf springs
are already rounded and need only to be sharpened for
use. The blade is sharpened on a single bevel (see illustration). Many leaf springs are naturally thinner
at the ends and sharpening can be done with a hand file.
If you can't find a piece already rounded, you will have
to modify a square-ended one on a grinding wheel. If you

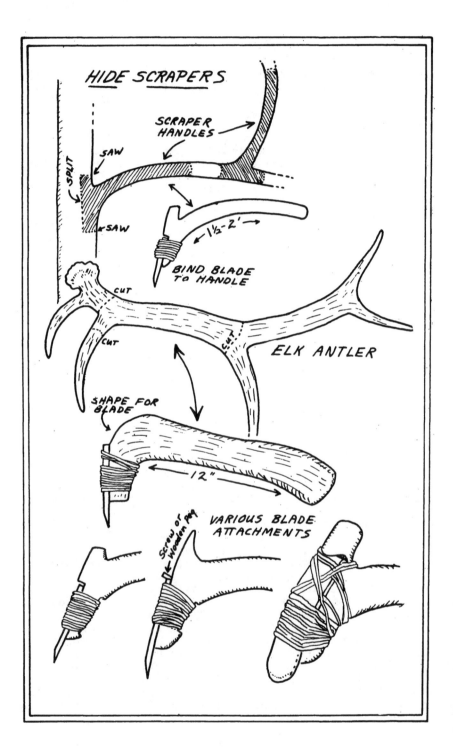

HIDE SCRAPERS

SCRAPER HANDLES

SPLIT

SAW

SAW

BIND BLADE TO HANDLE

1½-2'

CUT

CUT

CUT

ELK ANTLER

SHAPE FOR BLADE

12"

Screw or wooden peg

VARIOUS BLADE ATTACHMENTS

use an electric grinder, work slowly and carefully. Don't let the steel become too hot (from the friction) or it will "burn" (turn blue or black and become brittle) the cutting edge. This is more apt to occur once the edge is well-thinned and thus heats up faster. I keep a bucket of cold water (or in winter, some snow) handy to dunk the blade in frequently as I grind. The final, thinned cutting edge is best honed with hand files and oil stones. You can clamp the blade in a vise to hold it steady for final honing.

Almost any flat piece of steel can be fashioned into a workable scraper blade, but some hold a sharp edge longer. The scraping process tends to dull blades quickly, and it is imperative to keep your blade sharp while scraping. Sections cut from old sawmill saw blades, pieces of old farm equipment, reshaped cold chisels, etc., can all be used. If you cannot scrounge material for a blade, or don't have access to a grinding wheel, give the dimensions to a blacksmith (they're getting hard to find these days too!) or machine shop and they can make one up for you fairly cheaply (cost me three dollars for one cut from a giant old circular saw blade).

Because I teach aboriginal life skills courses in which making buckskin is one of the many primitive processes we do, I have had a chance to make and try out many hide scrapers. They go through some pretty rough use and I wanted some blades that held a good cutting edge longer than my old leaf spring blades (it takes students awhile to learn to sharpen blades with a file rather than dull them!). I went to a tool steel company, showed them a couple scrapers, explained my needs and asked them what they thought would work best for blades. What I purchased (for twelve dollars) were twelve rectangular sections four inches long (they cut them to that length for me), one and a half inches wide and a quarter inch thick of "Columbia Silvanite High Speed Woodknife Steel, Hardened Ready For Use, A.I.S.I. Type F 8." Now, parts of that description do not tell me alot, since steel technology remains pretty much above my stoneage consciousness, but the guy who showed me around was a black powder shooter who said this steel was extremely hard and held a good edge, but was still fairly easily ground for knife blades and such. He was right, and I have been quite satisfied with them. Each took over an hour to grind to the proper rounded and beveled shape, but the time was well spent; the blades stay sharp longer than any others I have used. I include this information just in case you want to invest in some super scraper blades!

SILVANITE SCRAPER BLADE
Natural Size

Single Bevel

1/4"

Rounded Cutting Edge

1 1/2"

Blade ends of 2 yew wood handled
hide scrapers. Left blade a modified
cold chisel, right cut from an old
cross cut saw blade.

THE DRY-SCRAPING PROCESS

You have a well-fleshed hide stretched symmetrically and dried in a sturdily constructed frame and you have a comfortable to grip scraper with a sharp, rounded blade--Right? You are now almost ready to begin the scraping process to remove the hair and grain (epidermal layer of skin) from the hide. Here are some things to do and to keep in mind before you actually begin.

First, inspect the flesh side of the hide for the location of any holes and badly scored areas. From the front, with a knife, trim the hair from around these holes so they <u>show up plainly</u>. It is a real bummer to be scraping along merrily and suddenly pop into, and greatly enlarge, an existing hole just because you didn't see it! Remember where the badly scored areas are and scrape more delicately there--it is better to leave some grain than to have the scores split open. As in fleshing, you will want to scrape with the direction of the scores, not across them.

Probably one of the hardest subjective decisions you will have to make as a novice buckskin maker is "How do I know when the hide is scraped enough?" I'll tell you what I can from my experience, but in the end it will be your own cumulative experiences that really teach you. All deerskins have similarities, but each also seems to have its own unique personality and characteristics. You should approach each hide with that in mind. Just when you think you have a good scraping system worked out, you'll encounter a hide that gives you nothing but trouble! Here are some brief observations I wrote while scraping a big buck hide several years ago.

"The hair and the first skin layer, a rich dark brown color, come off easily. Beneath that is a peppery looking layer--black dots and pockmarks of the basal portions of the hairs and hair follicles. Beneath that is a sort of yellowy dishwater colored layer which is very hard and seems to be sort of "pressed into" the hide. Beneath that is the almost pure white, fuzzy appearing layer that should be exposed over the whole hide surface when scraping is finished." A well scraped hide should be nearly uniformly white, except for blood-stained areas around bullet holes, etc.

Now, if all these layers came off cleanly and evenly, scraping would be an ease. But they don't. They come off unevenly, partly because you cannot always maintain the same degree of pressure and direction of scraping over the whole hide, partly because the different layers are stronger, tighter, thicker, etc. at different parts of the hide, partly because the hide itself is not of uniform thickness, partly because your scraper becomes less efficient when dull (the same as you or me!) and partly because, well, that's just the way deer hides are!

By the time you reach the point where there is only the yellow left (or grey on some hides) you may think you have already scraped too much (your arms will surely feel like it!), but you have to get that last layer of grain (or whatever it is) off if you want soft, fuzzy-surfaced (like suede) buckskin. To remove stubborn grain like this, you have to be very careful, yet scrape with alot of force. Resharpen your scraper and go back to work until the white layer finally starts to show through--it's under there somewhere! Hopefully, the illustration of animal skin in cross section will give you a better visual concept of skin structure and layering. While the diagram may not always coincide with what you perceive as you flesh, scrape, membrane or stake a hide, it should give you some helpful reference points. In some ways the diagram is kind of like a "deer skin road map"--you know it covers the right territory, but sometimes you find yourself on a backroad that the map doesn't show!

On most hides the grain is thickest on the neck, sometimes down the center of the back and thinner, but just as tough, on the rump. If you lightly scrape all the hair from a hide, you can see that these areas are often darker than the rest of the hide. Because of this thick grain, scraping often causes the surface to "washboard"--your scraper blade bounces and skips down the hide, forming parallel ridges and valleys much like what happens to the surface of a gravel road just before sharp curves and stop signs. If your hide starts to washboard (a common occurrence), stop scraping in that direction and scrape <u>with</u> the ridges, to shear them off. Say you are scraping downward, and the dreaded washboard appears; change to horizontal or even diagonal scraping and you should be able to eliminate them. Always resharpen your scraper when dealing with the washboard. Often it is a dull or loose scraper blade that causes it. A lot of times you will have to scrape problem areas several times in several different directions to remove most of the grain. The rump area is frequently the hardest for me. It often needs to be scraped paper-thin to remove all the grain, yet it amazingly later turns into some of the thickest buckskin on the whole hide.

Besides dealing with the grain, I believe the most

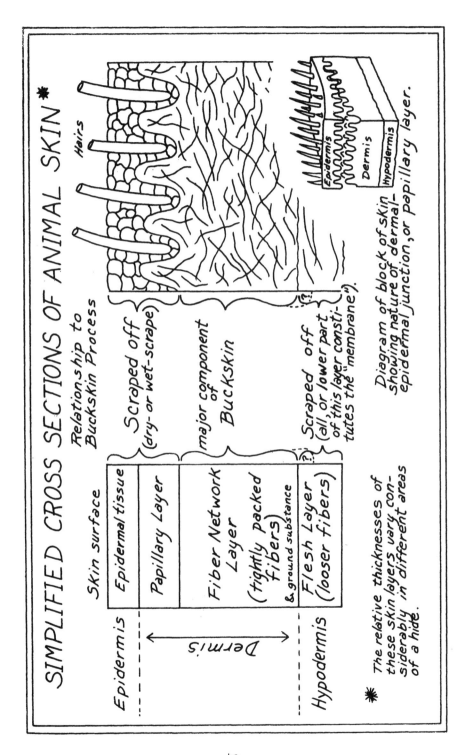

SIMPLIFIED CROSS SECTIONS OF ANIMAL SKIN *

Hairs

Relationship to Buckskin Process

Scraped off (dry- or wet-scrape)

major component of Buckskin

Scraped off (all, or lower part of this layer constitutes the "membrane").

Diagram of block of skin showing nature of dermal-epidermal junction, or papillary layer.

Epidermis
Dermis
Hypodermis

Skin surface

Epidermis	Epidermal tissue
Dermis	Papillary Layer
	Fiber Network Layer (tightly packed fibers) & ground substance
Hypodermis	Flesh Layer (looser fibers)

* The relative thicknesses of these skin layers vary considerably in different areas of a hide.

43

POPPING THROUGH!

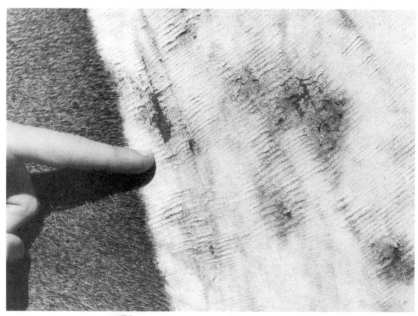

The dreaded "Washboard"

disturbing and frustrating problem you will encounter with this dry-scrape method is that of occasionally "popping through" the hide with your scraper. I call it popping through because that is the sound it makes on a tightly stretched hide. Most of the time there is good reason for it: your scraper is too dull; you are holding it at the wrong anle or are letting it slip sideways; you are pressing too hard on thin areas of the skin or where there are scores; you are scraping over a washboardy area, the scraper blade begins to bounce and finally breakes through; you scraped too much too fast in one concentrated spot, the skin got hot from friction and weakened; the skin is just plain weak in that spot anyway (possibly grease-burnt); you are making stabbing motions with the scraper instead of smooth, even strokes; you hit an unseen hole that you forgot to mark; you hit some other irregularity on the hide; maybe you are tired and frustrated or drinking too much beer while you work, ad infinitum. All of these have happened to me and more I'm sure that don't come to mind at this moment! Sometimes you pop through for no logical or discernable reason. That is just the way it is. Don't get down in the dumps and give up if you make some bad cuts. You can sew these up later and still end up with some mighty fine buckskin. When you see someone wearing real nice buckskin, you are seldom seeing entire hides; you are seeing pattern pieces that, for the most part, were fitted between or worked around those bad spots!

If you remain a little confused from all these words about the grain, how to identify it, how to best scrape it off, etc., you are not alone. I still encounter problems I've never faced before, and I still occasionally pop through. Above all, I hope my previous comments, and some of the following too, don't discourage you. Some hides scrape easy as pie (although, admittedly, I've never scraped a pie), and you may run through a batch free of any of the problems I have mentioned. You just have to accept each hide as it is and scrape it the best you can.

Keep files, whetstones & knife handy while you scrape a hide.

SCRAPING PROCEDURES

Now that I have mentioned many of the potential problems and tiny disasters you may encounter, you should be sufficiently paranoid to begin scraping your own deer hide! Here are some further tips and reiterations. The illustrations on scraping should help you to visualize some of these points.

Begin scraping at the top of the hide, at the neck. The hair is usually real thick here and you may want to first trim off a patch with your knife so the scraper can get a good bite.

For the most stability and control, I hold my scraper with one hand on the handle and the other cupped over the top, where the blade is affixed. My scraping motion is a smooth pull exerted by both hands. You should experiment with various grips to see what feels and works best for you; the neck of the hide is a good area for testing because it is thick.

The most efficient scraping technique I have found is illustrated for additional clarity. It is a moderate to long, smooth stroke in which the blade is already in downward motion when it lightly skims the hide just above the spot you intend to scrape. More pressure is then exerted, causing the blade to bite into the hide at the desired spot and to continue shearing off hair and grain for a couple to several inches. Pressure is gradually released as the blade is pulled away from the hide at the bottom of the stroke. The blade is in direct cutting contact with the hide during only the central part of its downward motion, and completely clear of the skin as you raise it for the next stroke. Rubbing the blade in both directions on the hide, "scratching around," is wasted energy, bad for the hide and dulls the blade. Of course, your strokes will be much shorter in delicate or problem areas.

While the blade is in cutting contact with the hide, the edge should be roughly perpendicular--at a ninety degree angle, a little less or more--to the skin surface. If you slant the blade too steeply into the hide surface as you scrape, it is likely to slice through whenever it hits an irregularity. <u>Don't get sloppy and forget this</u>!

Begin scraping lightly at first to get the feel of the scraper and skin. Over much of a typical hide (if, indeed there is such a thing) the hair and grain can be

46

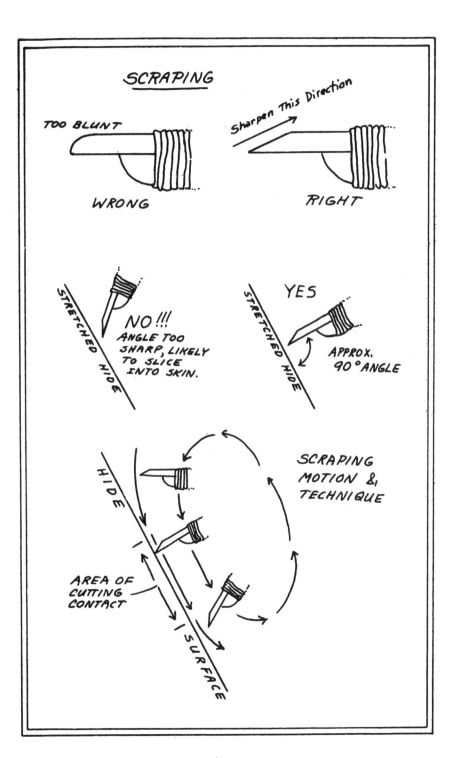

SCRAPING

TOO BLUNT

WRONG

Sharpen This Direction

RIGHT

STRETCHED HIDE

NO !!!
ANGLE TOO
SHARP, LIKELY
TO SLICE
INTO SKIN.

STRETCHED HIDE

YES

APPROX.
90° ANGLE

HIDE

SCRAPING
MOTION &
TECHNIQUE

AREA OF
CUTTING
CONTACT

SURFACE

removed at the same time with <u>single strokes of moderate pressure</u>, thus eliminating any need for scraping over the same spot two or three times; this finesse, however, comes with practice. To develop this, analyze your scraping strokes. Perfect ones may be few and far between at first, but when one does happen, notice how it feels and try to duplicate it.

There are basically two successful "plans of attack" for scraping a hide. One (and a good way to begin until you've become more experienced with scraping angles, pressure and motion) is to concentrate on removing mostly the hair from the whole hide first, then to go back over it, section by section, and scrape off the grain. The other is to work one area (a square foot or so) to completion. When it is mostly white and fuzzy (not still discolored or bristly from hair stubble and grain), move to an adjoining section and complete it; continue scraping in this way from top to bottom of hide. Either way is better than "random" or uneven scraping which beginners have a strong tendency to do. Random scraping creates furrows exposing the desired white layer juxtaposed with streaks and patches of hair and grain. In trying to remove these streaks, the white layer often gets unnecessarily rescraped and thinned, and the hide surface becomes less uniform. The least amount of scraping a hide must undergo (and still satisfactorily accomplish hair and grain removal) is most desirable.

After a little practice and after you get the feel of each individual hide, you can make long sweeps down the back and clean large areas rapidly. The grain will shear off in long, curled shavings. Remember to be much more careful and use shorter strokes around the edges and the thinner pit and groin areas of the skin. First trimming the hair from around the edges and tie slits is a good idea to prevent the scraper from sliding, slicing, slipping into them.

Initial scraping is best done with the direction of the hair from top to bottom of the hide, but you will encounter cowlicks in pit, groin and chest areas at each side of the skin that require more careful attention. Scraping too fast across these against the hair direction is just asking to pop through. Once the hair is removed, further scraping in different directions is less apt to cause problems.

Many deer hides have streak scars along the shoulders, back or rump (caused by sharp branches, thorns, barbed wire, etc., and occasionally representing claw marks left from an unsuccessful cat attack) which show as grooves of thickened grain and scar tissue. Don't try to scrape into or across these--they are apt to split open. Likewise, remember to scrape delicately

over surfaces badly scored from the flesh side. Sometimes the grain is the only thing holding these cuts together, and better to leave some grain than to have them
split open.

I emphasize, <u>keep your scraper blade sharp</u>! The
duller it becomes, the more pressure you apply to make
it cut and the greater the chance of pushing it right
through the hide. A dry, stretched hide can be very
brittle, especially if it has sat in hot sun for several
days. This is one reason I believe it is best to scrape
a hide as soon as possible after it dries. Keep medium
and fine whetstones and large and small flat files handy
while you scrape, and use them whenever your scraper begins to drag or rub and bounce along the hide surface
without getting a good bite. This dragging often ac-
centuates the washboard effect previously discussed.

Don't "get lost" in your scraping. Stop frequently,
stand back and view the area you are scraping as it re-
lates to the whole hide. If one spot is giving you
problems, leave it for awhile, scrape another, then come
back. Feel your cutting edge often. It should be sharp
enough so that you hesitate to slide your finger along
it. Always sharpen the blade by pushing file or stone
toward the cutting edge (see illustration). Brace the
blade and handle by kneeling or placing a foot on it,
clamp it in a vise, etc., so it doesn't wobble or vi-
brate as you sharpen it. After major sharpening of the
single bevel, use a fine whetstone to lightly clean any
"edge curl" or tiny filings that tend to accumulate on
the under surface of the cutting edge. These jagged
filings can snag or gouge into the hide. Don't allow
the angle of the cutting edge to become too blunt--this
happens frequently when a group of people is trading
different scrapers to try out or attempting to sharpen
blades without prior experience. When blades become too
rounded, rethin them on a grinding wheel. If a blade
becomes loose on a handle, rewrap it tightly.

While scraping, frequently brush off the hair and
grain shavings that tend to accumulate on the blade;
they hinder free cutting and make the blade slip along
the hide without getting a good bite. At the bottom of
every few downward strokes, I lightly brush the blade
against the hide just as I begin my upward lift for the
next stroke. This small, barely detectable motion
cleans the blade for succeeding strokes.

The more grain you can remove during the scraping
process, the nicer the hide surface will be on the finished buckskin. Too much grain left on will not allow
the skin to stretch, fluff and thicken adequately during
the staking process and will keep the skin stiff in
those spots as the hide dries. On the other hand,

Dry-scraping. Hair has been cut away from holes to make them easily visible & decrease possibility of inadvertently popping into them.

Flesh side, neck portion of a dried deer hide. Lighter area at left has been dry-scraped to partially remove the membrane. Note profusion of scores from improper skinning.

Dry-scraping. Note angle of scraper blades
to hide surface & stable grips on scrapers.

scraping too deeply into the white layer will thin the skin unnecessarily and leave scraper furrows on the surface, so there is a happy medium in there that you should strive for.

If you can't get all the grain off without fear of popping through, or if you really can't tell whether enough is removed, at least try to have it thinned and/or broken up enough so that it can stretch apart during the softening process. I have often noticed that the moment enough grain has been scraped from an area, the pressure of the scraper causes the skin to "give," to relax and stretch or "poof" a bit in that spot. This is most noticeable where the grain was thick and required repeated scraping.

Generally, I would advise this: <u>When in doubt, stop scraping</u>. Remember the location of the grainy spots and sand and work them extra thoroughly during softening. I have stopped scraping on some hides feeling for certain that I had left too much grain on, but had them soften up beautifully. Other times I thought I had done an excellent scraping job and had them turn out stiff in spots. Such is the folly of man trying to understand and explain everything in his world!

When you have finished scraping you can further work over remaining (or questionable) grainy spots with sandpaper backed on a sanding block or with gritty-surfaced but rounded sanding rocks. You must be careful, however, not to sand completely through the hide! For best results, place one hand lightly behind the spot you are sanding so you can feel if it is getting too thin. Sanding may not remove all remaining grain, but helps to thin it further and works well for smoothing washboardy areas. I used to sand hides at this stage, but now prefer to wait and do most sanding and smoothing with rocks during the staking process.

Sanding rocks are better than sandpaper because they work better (in my experience), last longer and don't cost money. I use pieces of sandstone, porous lava and several as yet unidentified but wonderfully gritty stones that came from a side canyon in Death Valley. When out in the countryside, keep your eyes peeled for potential sanding rocks, cart them home and try them out. Good rocks are extremely effective for removing the last bits of membrane during the staking process.

After scraping, some people turn the frame around and lightly scrape the flesh side with the hide scraper to begin breaking up the membrane. This is a difficult job to do thoroughly at this stage because scrapers, even sanding rocks, slip and slide on the dry, elusive membrane without biting in, and there is often no clearcut delineation between the membrane and the middle white

layer of skin. Sometimes I do this and sometimes I
don't, but most of the membrane will be removed during
the next step anyway.

To prepare for this, untie the hide from the frame
and resoak it in water. With the hair and grain gone,
it will soak up much faster than previously. Using
luke warm water will further speed soaking, but NEVER
SOAK A HIDE IN HOT WATER--it will cook! A good friend
stuffed his two best unblemished raw deer hides (they
had already been soaking a short while in a tub of cold
water, but this was in January...) into a five gallon
milk can, filled it up with hot tap water, sealed the
lid, put the can in his truck and drove down to my
place for a visit and a buckskin making session. The
next day we got the hide frames ready and opened the
can. Well, those still-warm hides were tender enough
to eat! We could simply pull them apart into little
pieces with our fingers. A lesson was learned and I
pass it along, so now there's no sense in you finding
this one out on your own!

The skin should be thoroughly saturated for the next
step, the membraning. Stretch and pull the skin in the
water to make sure it all gets soft. I usually let it
soak overnight and and work and stretch it again by
hand before removing it the next day. It now should be
ready for membraning.

53

MEMBRANING

Membraning (or more correctly de-membraning) is a
step I have incorporated into my buckskin process to
further insure that a hide will soften more easily
later. I believe that what I call membrane is the surface of the layer of connective and fatty tissue, the
hypodermis, on the flesh side of a skin. Along with
the grain, or epidermis, on the hair side, the hypodermis encases the middle layer of skin, the dermis (the
white surface you scraped down to), and keeps the dermal layer from stretching. When too much grain or membrane (especially both in conjunction) remain intact on
a skin, clamping and encasing that middle layer, adequate softening, stretching and fluffing are extremely
difficult to achieve. This membraning step helps to
eliminate that problem.

Make sure your dehaired and degrained hide is thoroughly wet, pliable and saturated with water. Remove
it from soaking and lay it over your fleshing beam,
flesh side up. Remember, the skin no longer has a "hair
cushion" to protect it, so a smooth beaming surface is
a must. Wetting a slightly less-than-smooth beam first
will help. The procedure for membraning is exactly like
that of fleshing, but the skin is more delicate without
the hair. Work carefully with your fleshing bar, maintaining the proper angle and systematically covering the
entire skin. The flesher will squeegee the water from
the skin as you work, so you should have no difficulty
determining what areas have or have not been covered.

The square edge of the flesher should shove off
varying amounts of membrane, from broad, thin sheets to
small bits. Sometimes you won't be able to discern if
anything that could be considered membrane is coming
off (perhaps much of it has already been removed by
fleshing and/or scraping), but it is important that you
go over the whole skin. It is best not to work in hot
sun, as it will dry out the skin too fast and prevent
or retard patches of membrane from coming off. Keep a
bucket of water handy for remoistening (rub it in) any
drying spots.

Wherever the membrane is sufficiently removed, the
skin will be much stretchier than before. Sometimes,
even this second beaming (fleshing was the first) may
not remove all the membrane, but usually at least serves
to break it up; what remains can be sanded off with

rocks while working the skin soft and dry later. Stiff areas due to insufficient membrane removal are the most common fault I see on buckskins produced by beginning buckskin makers.

Immediately after membraning is a good time to turn the skin over and use your flesher to go over any grainy areas or bits of hair left around the edges of the skin. By this stage, most remaining hair will slip off quite easily. It is especially good to go over any cuts or other holes in the skin to remove any adhering grain or membrane, so that once sewed closed, the immediate area around the holes will be less likely to stiffen up later.

During the membraning step, no matter which side of the skin you are working on, be extra careful of all scored areas.

SEWING UP HOLES AND CUTS

Immediately after membraning is a good time to sew closed any bullet holes or cuts made while scraping the skin. The hide should still be damp. If the edges of the holes you intend to sew begin to dry and stiffen, moisten them.

I work from the flesh side so the knots won't show on the outside. Fold the skin so the edges of each hole are together and sew them closed with simple overhand (whip) stitches. Other stitches, especially the "baseball" stitch, work well too. Oddly-shaped holes require a bit more imagination to close up, and it sometimes is a help to trim off ragged edges before sewing. Some gaping wounds can look fairly grotesque by the time you get them stitched up, but will adjust and flatten out when the skin is worked dry. If a hide has some bad scores that I'm sure will split open during softening, I also sew these closed as a sort of preventive maintenance. Make sure to tie beginning and ending knots tightly, as they will undergo alot of stress during softening.

Holes finely stitched with nylon beading thread, dacron or light linen shoemaker's cord are strong and will be nearly undiscernable on a finished buckskin, especially after it is smoked. If available, I prefer to use natural fiber thread because synthetics, particularly nylon, tend to enlarge the needle holes during softening. Quite often I will carefully mend with fine stitching all the holes within the major expanse of the hide, but do a faster, more cursory, job with larger needle, cord and stitches in marginal areas.

Remember to keep the areas moist that you are stitching; a needle makes a larger hole in dry or partly dry skin. Besides making the skin more esthetically pleas-

ing, sewing closed all the holes helps the skin to retain its proper shape during softening. You can decide
just how fine and thorough of a mending job you want to
do, but any efforts will contribute to a better finished
buckskin.

The skin is now ready for braining. It can be
stored in a plastic bag in the refrigerator until you
are ready.

OBTAINING BRAINS

If there is any secret other than diligence and hard
work to producing good buckskin, it rests in the brains!
Generally, one animal's brain is just the right amount
to tan its own hide, but I use more per hide if I have
them.

If you hunt your own deer, you will of course save
the brain. When you collect fresh hides from other hunters, try to get the brains too. Most of the time you
will acquire more hides than brains though, so you will
have to get brains from other sources. Any brains--cat-
tle, sheep, hogs, etc.--will do. One cow brain is
enough for two small to medium deer skins. For very
large deer hides I use a whole cow brain. Most often I
brain three to five hides at the same time, using a ra-
tio of roughly three cow brains for five deer hides.
Don't skimp on the brains if you don't have to.

Since brains are edible (considered a delicacy by
many), you can sometimes find them in the meat depart-
ments of some stores. There seem to be strange, red-
tape regulations regarding the butchering, processing
and sale of brains (no doubt stemming from the govern-
ment) in some areas, so most stores do not or cannot
stock them. On advance request, some stores will order
three, five or ten pound lots for you. Others simply
shake their heads and plead ignorance; they neither
have nor can get any brains! Should you know farmers or
ranchers who do their own stock butchering, be there at
the right time to get their brains. As with obtaining
hides, check out all potential sources.

If you want lots of brains for free (or if you've
failed in all other options), go to a slaughterhouse on
killing days, explain your needs and offer to cut the
brains from the heads yourself. With strange but benev-
olent looks, the workers will point to the barrels full
of heads, hooves, tails and guts and motion you to "go
to it!" (Don't first go to the office part--you'll only
confuse them--go directly to the killing floor.) I take
a meat saw, a tomahawk, a spoon and a sturdy plastic bag
or can with me. Ignore the blankly glazed eyes staring

up from those slippery skinned cow heads in the barrel and concentrate on business. I pull out a head, brace the slippery thing somehow on the floor, saw through most of the back of the skull, pry it open and spoon out the complete brain (often sawed in two) and top end of the spinal cord into my bag. Whew! One down. This is not a pleasant task nor a particularly appealing place to work, but they know me now and I can get all the free brains I can use, so I consider it worth the trouble (kind of like paying dues)! I take my newly acquired brain stash home, rebag each brain individually and freeze them for future use. A few hours before I intend to use them, I set them out to thaw. If you have no access to a freezer, you can can brains to preserve them or cut them into small globs and sun or oven dry them. Some people prefer to lightly boil them before drying, but some of the valuable oils are lost in the water. Some native peoples mashed and mixed the brains together with dry moss, molded the stiff mixture into a flat cake or ball and sun dried these to preserve them. To reconstitute, the ball was soaked and/or boiled in water.

THE BRAINING PROCEDURE

I prefer to soak my deer hides in a slurry of raw brains. Other buckskin makers prefer to simmer the brains in water for an hour or so before mashing them up. I can discern no difference (as far as effects) between raw or cooked brains for tanning.

In my researches, I have not yet found a well-documented explanation for the actual role the brains play in the tanning process, but I do know that they work (if you don't believe that a little bit of brain makes a difference, try working an unbrained deer skin soft and dry sometime!). One medical doctor told me he thought it was the lecithin in brains that helped. I've also heard it was amino acids. Well, with due respect for anyone else's ideas, my explanations for the effects of the brains on a hide follow: The brains provide natural oils which are readily and rapidly absorbed by the degrained and "demembraned" hide. These oils act as conditioners and lubricants for the skin fibers.

The dermis, or middle layer of skin which is the basis of buckskin, also contains a sticky, viscous fluid, a mucus-type of secretion which surrounds all the fibrous and cellular components of the dermis (refer to the diagram of animal skin in cross section). This liquid, sometimes termed "ground substance," acts in living skin as a natural lubricant (among other functions) for the dermal fiber network. When a skin is dried, however,

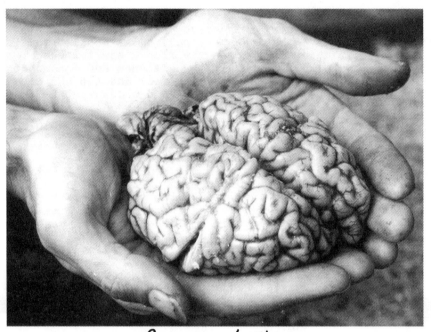

One cow brain.

Rubbing brain
"paste"
into a skin.

Working a skin into the
brain slurry.

58

this ground substance "sets up" like glue and, in combination with the tightly packed fiber network (among other things), is what makes a dried skin stiff. To constructively digress a bit and carry this further, pieces of skin may be boiled a couple to several hours (depends on skin size, condition, thickness, etc.) in water to extract the ground substance to make an extremely useful, though water-soluble, natural glue commonly used for backing bows with sinew, setting stone arrow points and fletchings solidly to shafts, etc. You can use dehaired pieces of hides or shavings from the scraping process to make your own glue. Boil the skin in water (don't start with too much water, but add more if/when necessary) until the water thickens considerably (to about the consistency of the commercial mucilage you used in gradeschool). Test your glue by dipping thumb and forefinger into it, allow them to dry enough to become tacky, then press them together tightly and hold for a minute or so. If you then have difficulty pulling thumb and finger apart, your glue is ready! It should be used while fresh or else preserved by freezing or drying; it will mold and/or rot if simply sealed and stored in its liquid state. To dry, continue heating it at a low temperature until most of the water has evaporated, then allow it to dry to a hard, translucent brown state. It will keep indefinitely and need only be reheated with a small amount of water for use.

But, returning to the braining procedure, perhaps the brains remove, dilute, neutralize or in some other manner counter the glue-like effects of the ground substance in the skin. At least some of the ground substance is removed during any tanning process to allow skins to soften. That the brains help to condition and soften a hide will be quite noticeable on your own hands as you work the hide in the brain emulsion. The brains also seem to lightly bleach or whiten a hide. During the staking process when the skin is worked dry and soft then, the brains and whatever their effects, coupled with your own continual physical manipulation of the skin, allow the skin fibers to loosen, slide easily against one another, expand and fluff up.

Properly speaking, buckskin is not really tanned at all. No known chemical changes occur in the skin or its fiber structure. In many chemical tans (chrome, sulphuric acid, etc.) the skins become soft partly because the chemicals weaken the skin structure. With real buckskin the overall softness comes, I believe, almost entirely from physical manipulation as aided by the lubricating and conditioning qualities of the brains. This process makes buckskin both softer and stronger than comparable chemically tanned deer skins. I would be hardpressed to document all of the foregoing assertions (although the existence and characteristics of the ground substance and skin layers are recorded in literature), so consider most of them only my own theories until you can decide for yourself.

I never thought I would espouse the use of a modern electrical gadget, but the fastest and most efficient way to prepare the fresh or now-thawed brains is in an electric blender (egg or other beaters and hand-mashing run a distant second and third). Dump the brains into the blender, push the "Liquify" button and presto, you instantly have a thick, pink "brainshake!" I figure the more the brain is homoginized, the more oil that is freed to soak into the skins. When I lived isolated and blenderless in the southwestern Oregon mountains, I first cleaned away blood clots and the tough separating membranes in the brain for easier hand-mashing, but I don't bother to do this with the blender.

When the brain is thoroughly blended, I fill the blender to the top with hot or boiling water and re-blend. This still-thick pink glop I pour into a bucket, add more water while stirring vigorously until I have roughly a gallon of brain slurry, or enough to cover however many hides I intend to soak. When the mixture has cooled to warm (not hot!), I slowly work each skin into it, making certain that the sudsy liquid reaches and is worked into all parts of the skin by stretching and pulling it while sloshing it around.

Some buckskin makers leave skins in the brain slurry for as few as twenty minutes. I usually let them soak overnight, resloshing them before I go to bed and again in the morning before removing them. Brains (just like brain jokes!) have a habit of getting real ripe real fast, however, and I am not sure there is any real benefit in leaving hides in them for extended periods, providing they are thoroughly saturated and manipulated initially. When you first slosh a hide into the brains, you will feel a sudden, major change in the skin consistency, a slipperiness and softening as the oils soak in. This may be all that is necessary. In my experience, there is no adequate substitute for brains in preparing buckskin. No neatsfoot oils, fish oils, soft soaps, etc., quite "do the thing" that brains do, but you can use these substitutes (they are better than nothing) if obtaining brains is impossible. Personally, I think that is improbable--you should be able to use your own brain to locate some others--even if it means collecting road-kill squirrel heads until you have enough!

I believe that soaking skins in the brains and water mixture does the most thorough braining job, but in a primitive or survival setting, without containers, you can spread a skin out (preferably on a clean surface), make a goopy, hand-mashed brain paste (add a little water if possible) and just smear this all over both sides of the skin. Then roll the skin up into a small, tight wad and knead it like a hunk of bread dough to help distribute the brain oils, allowing them to "strike through" all parts of the skin. Then place your wad of skin in a plastic or paper bag or any other convenient wrapping and let it sit in a warm place for several hours to further help the oil penetration. I satisfactorily brained most of my first hides this way.

When you remove a hide from the brain slurry (or unroll it after brain-pasting), you can proceed in a couple different ways. One is to hang or drape the dripping skin on a line and let it bake completely dry (make sure all edges dry thoroughly too) in the hot sun. Once dry, it can be stored until you plan to soften it. Vermin love dried, brained hides, so be sure to seal or store it in a protected spot. Some written accounts and friends say that sun drying further helps penetration of brain oils. This may be true, especially for pasted hides, but doesn't really seem to matter. The drying step is a convenient option I sometimes use when I brain several hides together and can't work them all dry at once or when I need an example of a hide at this intermediate stage in the process for a demonstration, but for hides that are soaked in brains, I don't believe it is a necessity. I can detect no noticeable benefit in the finished buckskin. Dried, brained hides must, of course, be thoroughly resoaked in plain water until again pliable, then wrung out in preparation for working them soft and dry in the frame. Freshly brained hides can also be frozen and stored until needed.

Let us proceed, however, with a skin taken directly from the brain slurry; it must be wrung out to remove as much excess moisture as possible.

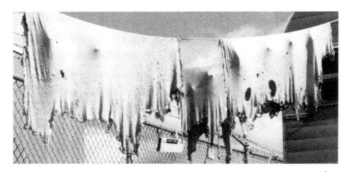

Freshly brained skins hung to dry in the sun. They are propped open with sticks for free air circulation.

WRINGING

Wringing is the important preparatory step to working a brained hide dry and soft. Wringing serves two
main functions: It removes excess moisture from the
skin, thus reducing the length of time needed to work
it dry, and it begins to stretch the hide. I should
mention that in many buckskin processes a hide is wrung
both before and after braining. The idea is that wringing before braining stretches the skin fibers, opens the
pores and generally allows more thorough brain satura-
tion. In my process, two wringings would certainly not
hurt, but I don't believe that the first is really necessary.

A good healthy skin should withstand vigorous wringing. Occasionally during wringing the stitching on
poorly mended holes may rip out; these should be resewed.
Well-mended holes should remain intact. If a hide has
been grease-burnt, is badly scored or otherwise weakened
(perhaps thinned too much during scraping, etc.) it may
also pull apart in those places. This is the chance you
take, and remedy as best you can.

Variations of wringing techniques are numerous and,
again, you should experiment to determine which works
best for you. My standard (and very thorough) wringing
procedure is as follows (refer also to correspondingly
numbered illustrations): 1) Lay the skin out flat on a
clean surface. I always put the flesh side up, but it
probably makes no difference. 2) Beginning at a front
or rear leg, fold in the uneven edges and tightly roll
the skin up toward the center, not to a straight mid-
line from neck to tail, but to a diagonal line from one
front leg to opposite rear leg. 3) Do the same with
the other side. Now you have two parallel rolls of skin
connected along the bottom like a scroll. The skin is
rolled diagonally (on a bias) because it stretches more
that way, although this too may not really matter. 4)
Grab one end of the scroll (both rolls together), step
on the other end to hold it down and twist it several
turns. 5) Pick up both ends of the twisted hide and
loop it around a smooth, stationary bar, limb or pole.
6) Tuck and work several inches of each loose end into
the folds of the other so you have a continuous twisted
skin hoop. You may have to partly loosen the folds to
deeply tuck each end in. 7) Insert a smooth, sturdy
two-foot stick (a staker works fine) through the skin

loop, pull tautly (keeping the tucked ends from slipping out)and twist the skin up tightly by turning the
stick as many turns as it will go one way. Pull concertedly on the stick as you twist to stretch the skin
and allow you to complete more turns before the skin
"knots up." Water should stream out. When dripping
slows or ceases, blot the skin with an old towel. Un-
twist to the beginning point (skin loop), revolve the
skin a quarter turn around the stationary bar so the
stress and contact points will be different, and re-
twist as before, but in the opposite direction. Nearly
all the water will be squeezed from the skin by this
method. It is good to hold or bind the wringing stick
in place for a few minutes once the skin is twisted up
to its tightest point so more water has a chance to
drip out. Any still-soggy areas on the surface of the
twisted skin can again be further dried by patting and
squeezing them with the towel. If a hide has been well
scraped and membraned, you should notice water and air
bubbles squeezing through all visible surfaces (much as
you used to squeeze water and air through a washcloth
when a kid taking a bath).

An alternative, simpler wringing method is effective, though not quite as thorough. Run one smoothed,
one inch diameter stick or bar through all slits across
the top of the neck skin. Have another person hold this,
or tie it to something immovable. Run a second stick
through several slits at the ends of each rear leg.
Pull this stick to stretch the hide out and fold into
the center all loose edges, front legs, sides of the
skin, etc. Maintain tension on the hide, keep the
folded-in parts from falling out or flapping loose, and
twist up the skin with the stick running through the
hind legs. As in the first wringing method, keep tension on the skin as you twist and twist it up as
tightly as you can. Blot wet areas with a towel and
twist the skin in the opposite direction also. One
problem with this method is that you may occasionally
tear out some of the slits.

After wringing by either of these methods, a skin
will be tightly compressed and rather difficult to pull
back apart. At this stage on the first hide I ever tanned, I thought for certain I had totally destroyed it--
I could visualize no way this tight wad of damp skin
was going to become fluffy white buckskin (but it did)!
The skin must be untwisted, unrolled and hand-stretched
back to its original shape for tying into the frame.
If your hide has been prepared well and if the
wringing thorough, it should have the nearly uniform
consistency of a damp washcloth. Any areas remaining
really wet will appear bluish or grey and, of course,

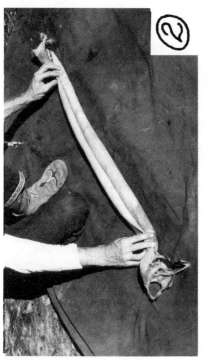

WRINGING

6

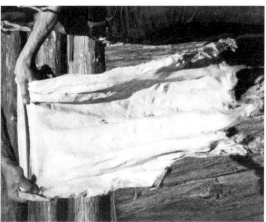

8

5

7

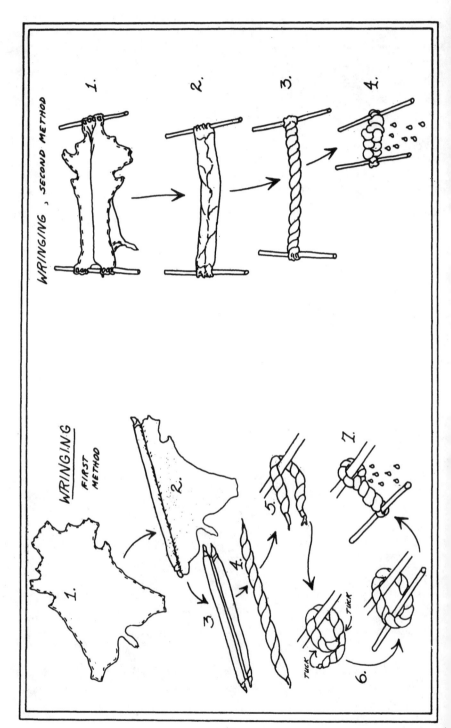

WRINGING, SECOND METHOD

1. 2. 3. 4.

WRINGING
FIRST METHOD

1. 2. 3. 4. 5. 6. 7.

TUCK TUCK

66

feel wetter. Sometimes these remaining wet areas will
signify some impermeable grain or membrane and sometimes
they are only the result of uneven wringing. Further
blot them with a towel, keep your eyes on them during
softening and work them over extra well.

In a pinch, you can simply wring and twist moisture
from a skin by hand, but this is less satisfactory. The
wringing is uneven and many areas remain saturated.
Should you have a skin that, because of its thinness or
profusion of mended holes, you feel will not stand up
to a vigorous wringing, you can wring it by hand first,
then blot much of the moisture from it as you would a
wool garment. Spread it out on dry towels, cover with
more towels and roll it up. Squeeze the roll thoroughly
with your hands or smash and knead it on the floor or
ground with your knees.

If you will be working your hide dry in an extremely
hot, arid climate, more moisture left in the skin may be
desirable (to give you more· time to tie the skin back
into the frame without portions of it drying too fast
before you can work them). Likewise, in a more humid
environment, the drier (but not dried to stiffness) the
hide after wringing, the better. Concerning factors
such as these, and so many others in the buckskin process, please remember that I can only give you guidelines from my own experiences; I can't make your subjective evaluations for you. There is much room for
trial and error in the buckskin process. To become a
proficient buckskin maker, you must apply your own common sense and intuition to your own unique circumstances.

With the skin thoroughly wrung, you are immediately
ready to begin the staking process. If necessary, you
can store the skin by refrigerating (short-term) or
freezing it until you are ready.

THE STAKING PROCESS
Working The Skin Soft And Dry

If you have not made buckskin before, nor seen anyone else accomplish this step in particular, I doubt that I can adequately prepare you for it--not so much for the difficulty of the task, but for the rewards. I shall endeavor to do both.

First, there are two major systems for working a buckskin dry and soft--mostly by hand or mostly in a frame. Each has its own benefits and drawbacks, advocates and critics, but both were used extensively in aboriginal America. I shall deal mostly with the in-frame method here.

Staking is the final step in the buckskin process before smoking. It is the step in which the damp, clammy, occasionally odoriferous and generally unpleasant hide is "magically" transformed into a dry, soft, fluffy, warm and supple white buckskin--your very own buckskin! I never tire of causing this unbelievable transformation to occur. This is the step that makes you feel all the previous work leading up to it was really worth it.

Staking is arduous (you'll discover muscles you didn't know you had), often time-consuming (allot several hours; in fact, for your first time around, I'd suggest leaving the day open-ended) and frequently a bit frantic (racing to tie the skin into the frame before thinner portions dry and stiffen too much, keeping track of the condition of the entire skin while concentrating on specific areas, both at the same time, etc.). During staking you can correct some past mistakes and/or make up for some inadequately completed previous steps (one more chance to remove remaining grain and membrane).

The only way you can stake a hide too much is to initially stretch it too tightly in the frame, then keep retightening it as it loosens, thus forcing the skin fibers to separate rather than to have "rebound" room. They need slack to stretch, then spring back and fluff. With proper tying, the more staking, the softer the buckskin. Here are some other things to do and remember before you actually tie your skin into the frame and begin.

STAKING TOOLS

The specialized staking tools (stakers) are much simpler to make than your scraper and flesher. When it gets down to it, almost any sturdy stick will suffice, but most of mine are modified one and a half to four foot long wooden poles one to two inches in diameter with chisel-like wedge or oar shaped working ends (see illustrations). These were first whittled and planed to rough shape, then sanded very smooth.

Stakers can be fashioned from any kind of wood not inherently rough or splintery, although dense, fine-grained hardwoods are best. I was taught that dogwood was the very best because the chisel-shaped end stayed sharp, yet became very smooth and polished and wore evenly. Don't feel cheated if you have no dogwood though; I have equally functional stakers of yew, serviceberry, mountain mahogany, chokecherry, juniper, Oregon ash and even some quickly made ones of pine and fir that work okay--they just have to be resmoothed and reshaped more often. Broken hickory axe, maul or other handles (any length) are easily reshaped into stakers and work excellently. You can even smooth up an old wooden oar and use it.

The most important part of a staker is the slightly flared, round-cornered, wedge or chisel-shaped working end, but the handle section should be well-smoothed and comfortable to grip or else you will acquire blisters muy pronto! More than a few times I've ended up with bloody hands, but a super soft buckskin to show for them. I think it best to have at least a couple stakers on hand, one narrow-width (about one inch) and a wider one with more flare (two or three inches). The narrower one is real good for stretching the skin close to the edges and breaking up tight areas of the skin, the wide one good for overall manipulation.

Besides a couple stakers, have your hide scraper, knife, sanding rocks of various "grits" and shapes (or sandpaper and sanding block) all handy before you begin.

STAKING CONDITIONS

The time it takes you to work a hide dry and soft can vary considerably. I've done it in less than an hour (light skin in hot sun) and longer than twelve hours (large hide inside an unheated room). Average drying time outside in dry air and mostly sunny weather is two to three hours, inside with a direct heat source (wood stove), three to five hours. These times are only rough averages from my own experiences; yours may vary.

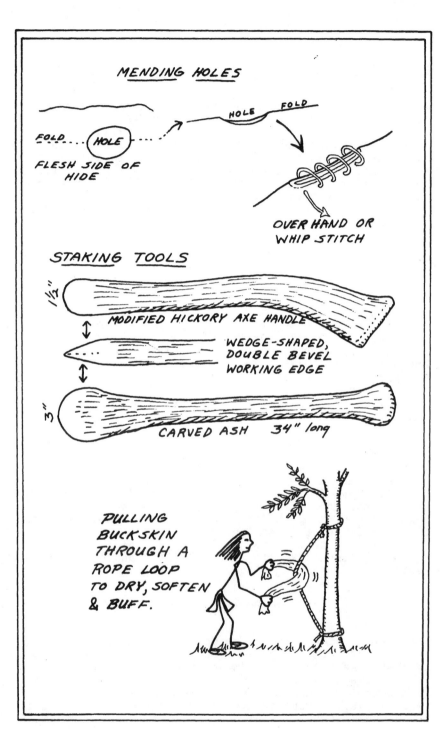

MENDING HOLES

FOLD .... (HOLE)
FLESH SIDE OF
HIDE

HOLE   FOLD

OVER HAND OR
WHIP STITCH

STAKING TOOLS

1/2"

MODIFIED HICKORY AXE HANDLE

WEDGE-SHAPED,
DOUBLE BEVEL
WORKING EDGE

3"

CARVED ASH   34" long

PULLING
BUCKSKIN
THROUGH A
ROPE LOOP
TO DRY, SOFTEN
& BUFF.

Generally, the more continuously and concertedly a hide is worked, the faster it will dry. Part of the time you will be "working your butt off" and during other parts you will be able to take short breaks. You will soon learn "What you must do When" and "When you can afford to do What!" If these remarks are not clear, muse on them as you work your first hide dry!

Staking is most efficiently and pleasantly accomplished outdoors on a nice day in a spot where you can move the frame back and forth between sun and shade if necessary. It can be done inside, but always seems to take longer. I stake many hides indoors during winter (some sort of workshop with wood heat is best), however, so don't let foul weather deter you.

What follows is an "ideal" version of my standard approach to staking a hide. You can take whatever seems important and plug it into your own situation: In the morning of what appears to be a warm, sunny day, either in the shade or before the sun hits, I tie the freshly wrung hide into the frame. Morning coolness and shade prevent too-rapid drying while I'm tying. I then "get to know" the skin, working it slowly with a staker and my hands, noting potential problem areas, etc. I work every part of it until it is looser and stretchy all over, though still quite damp. Once I think I have "control" of it, I move it into the sun and work it nearly continuously until it is dry and soft. During the working I freely switch from hands to stakers to sanding rocks to hide scraper occasionally--whatever means seems most appropriate for the whole hide or any particular spot on which I'm concentrating.

The sun can be your ally or your foe--learn to use it to your advantage. Most hides done in the above format will take about two hours of working to get them into the "safe" zone (where they won't appreciably stiffen if not further worked). Often you will have to work a few damper spots longer, especially the neck and each side of the rump, after most of the skin is already dry and soft.

STAKING PROCEDURES

You have completed the wringing and have stretched the skin back out by hand to its original shape. Now tie it back into the frame in the same manner as before, original hair side out, neck first, then rear legs, etc. Again, make sure the skin is positioned symmetrically and tied evenly in the frame. Remember to tie it securely; both skin loops and rope ties will undergo much movement and stress during staking. Notice, now that the grain and membrane are mostly gone and the hide has been wrung, the skin is slightly larger. Do not stretch the skin too tightly in the frame. It should be taut, but not as taut as you could tie it. After tying (but before working it) the surface should neither sag nor be drum tight. Achieving the proper tension will come with experience. Make sure the frame is sturdy (staking really gives a frame a workout) and positioned so you can easily get behind it or turn it around or sideways when necessary.

Fasten the ropes securely! Knots are better for most ties this time around. The "friction" ties I use when stretching a hide for scraping tend to work loose when the skin and ropes are in nearly constant motion. Expect a few ties to break loose during staking. If key ties rip out, ones whose absence allows the skin to assume a shape other than as first positioned in the frame, cut new slits and retie them.

If any areas seem to be drying out too fast (the drier they get, the whiter they become) while you are still tying, work them briefly but rapidly, then finish tying as quickly as you can. Always do the major "center the hide" ties first, then complete the others.

Usually the areas that tend to dry fastest are the thinner skinned pit and groin regions near the legs at each side of the skin. Here is a good maneuver for rapidly softening small areas. Place one open palm against the back side (behind the frame) of the spot to be worked, the other palm against the front. Press and hold both palms together, clamping the hide between them, and rapidly move the skin in circular motions, up and down, back and forth, pulling and pushing to keep the skin in motion, stretching and loosening it. This maneuver is excellent for breaking loose any grain or membrane and for working a skin soft right out to the ties. Use this method (and any other grabbing, pulling, stretching, etc. that seems to work) first on the rapidly drying spots, but eventually on as much of the hide as you can reach. The more buckskin I do, the more I rely on this "palm against palm" technique for softening.

Also, as one of the initial staking procedures, poke the fairly taut skin all over with one of your stakers. Begin lightly (perhaps depressing the hide surface an inch or two), and as the skin stretches, loosens and dries more, you can increase the OOOMPH behind your push with the staker. At first, you will notice the staker indents only a small spot right where it is pushed into the hide. As you continue poking the hide all over, you will notice a much larger area of the skin stretching toward any one spot you push. This shows that the skin fibers are loosening as desired. Especially at first, don't poke too hard in thin spots, scored areas or mended holes.

While the skin is still appreciably damp, don't rub it with the staker; rubbing comes after the skin is a bit drier. The hide becomes stronger and more elastic as it dries. Toward the end of staking when you are really leaning into the skin with your staker, the whole skin will stretch and move toward any one spot that you push. Remember to begin lightly, though, and work up to this stretchiness.

After the initial ten or fifteen minutes of "palm-rubbing" and poking, the skin will have stretched, loosened and sagged considerably in the frame. This is desirable as long as key ties are not ripping out and allowing the skin to become misshapen. The slack better allows the skin to stretch with each staking push, then rebound when the staker is released. If you feel there is too much slack, go ahead and retighten some of the ties, but make sure to do it evenly and keep the hide in its natural shape (a skin tied crookedly and forced to soften, dry and temporarily "set" in an unnatural shape can cause all sorts of problems when you later notice your moccasins, shirtsleeves, etc., are twisting, shrinking, lengthening, shortening, etc., as the skin slowly returns to its natural shape).

I emphasize, staking is not simply a random procedure. Once the whole hide is looser and stretchy, the object is to keep it in nearly continual motion as it dries. This motion prevents damp areas from setting up, becoming stiff. Damper and problem areas must be worked more concertedly, but don't forget to frequently stretch the entire skin and keep track of the progress of both sides.

As the skin becomes drier, the staker can be pushed into it with greater force and rubbed along the surface, also with great pressure. You will have to determine just how much pressure to exert in specific areas during any given phase of the staking process as you gain experience, but most beginners tend not to push hard enough. I usually don't rub with the staker until the skin surface begins to get smooth (meaning the staker slides easily along it, rather than "jerkily" from too much remaining moisture which creates more drag from friction). I normally don't rub the staker back and forth, but apply pressure to long, controlled downward strokes. Strong staking pressure combined with rapid back and forth rubbing may be necessary and is effective on rump and neck, which are thicker, retain moisture longer and require more forceful staking.

With all the forceful contact between staker and

Final stages of staking a buckskin. Note the force with which the staker is pushed into & rubbed down the skin. (Dick Jamison photo)

Even the best laid plans.....
This hide simply ripped
apart during staking, possibly due to prior greaseburning.

Staking A Buckskin
(Dick Jamison photo)

hide, it is important to keep your staker end smooth; a wayward splinter or rough spot can gouge into the skin. It helps to turn the frame around and stake the flesh side also. On most hides I'll work each side about equally. The main thing is to keep track of both sides-- don't just become so involved with one that you forget the other. Always keep the whole hide in mind.

In my courses staking is often a frantic process with two or three people working on each hide, and I'm frequently asked "How can one person do this alone when three people have so much trouble?" My response is that I believe it is actually easier for one person to keep track of a whole hide, moving freely and systematically to cover all areas of both sides. More people get in each other's way and frequently no one can maintain an overall perspective. With a little coordination, though, two people can do a good job.

Use sanding rocks, sanding blocks or your hide scraper to go over grainy or membrany spots. These tend to stretch less, dry more slowly, remain "tight" and not adequately fluff and thicken, so are easily spotted. Two or three times during the process it is a good idea to rub the entire surfaces of both sides with a sanding rock. This fluffs the surface more and especially allows deep-seated moisture to evaporate faster. The skin surfaces, particularly the flesh side, tend to kind of "glaze over" and trap moisture from escaping if not sanded periodically. Sanding is a good finishing touch when the hide is thoroughly dry also. Sand especially hard around tie loops; unseen membrane likes to lurk there!

Mostly by hand, work carefully over thin areas, mended spots and scores, especially at first when the skin is dampest. These will strengthen and withstand more stress as the skin becomes drier. Occasionally your staker may pop through one of these thin areas, but you can mend it before smoking.

Don't slack off in your staking efforts just because the hide is beginning to soften, fluff, dry and thicken. If anything, increase your staking activity. Pull the hide in all directions from all the edges (turn the frame sideways or upside down as needed). Wiggle the tie loops. Rub and poke and slide and press your fingers and hands in all directions over the hide. Really stretch and distend the skin as you do this. Bounce your whole body weight, hands outstretched, against the hide, and spring back off it. Work the hide with every conceivable softening measure or manipulation you can think of. Work like your life depended on every inch of that skin becoming thoroughly soft. If you want a superb buckskin, you have to jump into staking wholeheartedly!

Perseverance, dedication, improvisation and developing finesse are keys to good staking (I'm sure there are more!). Make up your mind that no part of the skin will remain stiff, then follow through with that plan using whatever means are necessary. You can take short breaks, sometimes five or ten minutes toward the end of staking, but do not let the skin stiffen while you eat lunch, tune up your car, etc. After you have done several hides, you'll learn when and when not to take a break. The most common mistake ("miss-stake"!) beginners make is not staking hard enough (especially increasing the intensity as the skin becomes drier), thoroughly enough or long enough. Toward the end of staking, I lean into a hide with all my weight.

As the skin dries it will whiten and thicken considerably. When dry, it will feel warm to the touch (press your cheek against it to tell); any spot or area still damp will feel cool and should be concertedly further worked. Both sides of a finished buckskin should be soft and supple. The surface of the flesh side is usually fluffier than the hair side (probably because the fibers of the hypodermis layer, some of which usually remain on a buckskin, are less densely packed than those of the dermis. A friend who wet-scrapes his hides and usually works them dry and soft by hand through a wire loop, buffs the skins so thoroughly and vigorously that most of the fluffy hypodermis is removed deliberately).

I prefer to work a skin totally dry in the frame, but occasionally by necessity or choice (darkness, rain, company just came, gotta run, etc.) I remove it while portions may still be lightly damp and pull it the rest of the way dry by hand. This is most easily done with two or more people standing opposite or in a small circle, each holding on to an edge of the skin and working out a rhythmic pattern of leaning back (to stretch the skin) and then bouncing forward. This not only stretches and softens the hide well, but frequently becomes hilarious as opposite partners try to maintain the rhythm. Sometimes a system of counting helps to coordinate the leaning back--rebounding sequence. Have fun!

One person can rapidly pull a skin back and forth through a rope or wire (heavy-duty) loop affixed at two different points to a tree, fencepost, wall, etc. I often do this as a final buffer for hides worked dry in the frame. A deer hide naturally varies in thickness from one part of the skin to another, but a well-staked hide should end up basically white, soft, supple and stretchy all over. If any spots remain slightly stiff or "crinkle" when bent. they were not worked enough. Sand or

Pulling deer hides dry & soft. These buckskins have been staked mostly dry in
frames first, then removed & given a final
workout by hand.

pick off any grain or membrane and sometimes, with
vigorous, concerted, localized rubbing and manipula-
ting, you can still soften these spots, even with the
hide basically dry. Stiff spots or not, if you are generally satisfied with the hide, go ahead and smoke it.
Once the skin is made into clothing, worn, washed and
just plain used awhile, stiff spots will eventually soften.
     A skin worked dry in a frame generally turns out a
little larger than one worked entirely by hand. Hand-
worked hides sometimes end up a little thicker (no tie
ropes to prevent them from shrinking more). In my experience, hand-worked hides tend to be "paunchy" in the
middle, with irregularly stretched edges. They do not
lay out flat, thus making the cutting of pattern pieces
more difficult. Many people have workable systems for
hand-softening though, and like wet-scraping, it is simply another way to achieve the same end, buckskin. Adequately covering both of these alternatives is just not
within the range of my experience (yet!) nor the scope
of this booklet.
     Staking is a multifarious process. I hope I have
introduced it well enough here so that, even have I left
out some useful further hints, you can get the major
ways and means down. I have reiterated many points I
feel are extremely important. Eventually, the methodology of staking (and all the other steps in the buckskin
process) will become second nature for you. After successfully bringing a hide this far through the buckskin
process, you are obviously capable of common sense
thinking and improvising to best suit your own needs.
     When staking is completed and the hide is dry and
soft, I untie it from the frame and trim off the outside
rim of often still-damp tie loops. Some people prefer
to leave them on until the smoking process is completed
(and some people have scraped and membraned and softened
the loops so well that they don't trim them at all!).
It's your choice.
     Hey! You have made buckskin! The finishing step is
to smoke it.

SMOKING

Smoking is the final step in the buckskin process (other than creating your own unique clothing). To my way of thinking, smoking is a necessary step if you want functional, durable buckskin for everyday wear, but many native groups prefered white, unsmoked buckskin for ceremonial dress. Many modern natives and traders place a higher value on white skins. While I have seen many unsmoked skins for sale at various trading posts from Wind River, Wyoming (forty to sixty dollars each, 1973) to Taos, New Mexico (ninety five dollars each, 1975), I have yet to see a smoked one. To me, an unsmoked buckskin is simply unfinished. Let me explain.

The most obvious effect of smoking is that of coloring a hide. Generally, the longer a skin is smoked, the darker yellow, tan, brown, etc., it becomes; actual color depends largely on the material(s) used to produce the smoke. The most important effect of smoking is that of allowing a skin to dry soft, even after repeated wettings and washings. Actually, a thoroughly wet smoked buckskin left to dry untouched will stiffen as it dries, but is easily resoftened by shaking it a few times and briefly pulling and stretching it with the hands. An unsmoked hide must be thoroughly reworked soft and dry each time it becomes wet (though the process is easier and shorter than the original staking); left to dry untouched, it will dry stiff and remain so. Perhaps this stiffening is the result of lingering ground substance (previously described in THE BRAINING PROCEDURE) in the dermis. This drying stiff factor alone makes unsmoked buckskin useless (or, at best, extremely impractical and uncomfortable) for standard wilderness clothing. I have often humorously pictured an entire native camp sitting around resoftening their unsmoked ceremonial buckskin outfits after an unexpected rainstorm! Barring unplanned wettings, unsmoked buckskin was generally cleaned by rubbing in finely powdered white gypsum, clay or diatomaceous earth. These lightly abrasive substances tended to "lift out" the dirt.

Besides being more versatile, then, a smoked skin is distasteful to clothes moths (as long as the effects of smoking are still evident, usually through several washings), whereas moths positively relish unsmoked skins. Also, smoked buckskin does not show dirt like white skins (you can appear in town in filthy buckskins and,

as long as you don't reek, no one will know the difference because very few "reglar folks" know what buckskin
is supposed to look like!). I have read of or heard
several other assertions concerning the beneficial effects of smoking hides, but just plain discount some and
cannot verify others from my own experience.

What smoking actually does to the skin I can't de-
clare with absolute certainty either, but the smoke (containing various pitchy or oily substances) readily permeates the soft buckskin, filling or lining the skin
pores and coating or permeating the skin fibers. Because pitch is water resistant and not readily water
soluble, it keeps the skin fibers free from adhering to
each other; it prevents them from "setting up" as they
dry. So, tentative as this explanation may be, suffice
it to say, smoking a hide is important because it works.
Do it!

SMOKING PROCEDURES

I shall describe my current smoking set-up and procedures, and the illustrations should give you some additional ideas and variations. There are lots of things
to do and watch for in the smoking process, but nothing
so involved as in staking.

Smoking is an outside job. It requires an open
fire and, naturally, produces alot of smoke. I have
done it in city backyards, but if you don't want the local fire department (and everyone else who follows them)
breathing down your neck, or the owner of Fang's orien-
tal restaurant just down the block running over waving
his arms and hysterically screaming that your smoke is
flowing directly into his kitchen doorway and ruining
the delicate flavors (ala monosodium glutamate) of his
gourmet cuisine, you better do it out in the country.
It's nicer out there anyway!

I have a small pit approximately one foot wide and
deep in which I build a roaring little fire to produce
a good bed of coals several inches deep. I also have a
small hole punched with an iron rod through the dirt
which angles from the ground surface about a foot and a
half from the pit to the bottom of the pit. This is the
draft hole. When I plug the top end, the fire slows
down; when I leave it open, the fire flares up. I use
this hole to regulate the amount of smoke and to make
sure the coals stay alive during smoking.

My favorite materials for producing smoke are rotten
Douglas fir (the really rotten, punky, often powdery
stuff inside rotting stumps and logs) and freshly-picked
green juniper boughs. Both materials produce a thick,

billowy bluish smoke which first turns a hide a yellow-
ish tan, then deepens it to a nice buckskin brown. Both
have distinctively pleasant aromas. I have also used
green willow leaves (nice rich brown color, mediocre
smell), rotten ponderosa pine (rich yellow-brown, nice
smell), sagebrush foliage (nice tan-brown, nice smell)
and a few times rotten and green vegetation of unknown
derivation. Cottonwood is favored by many (leaves and/
or rotten wood), and I am sure each aboriginal buckskin
maker believed that whatever he (usually she) used was
better than what anyone else used. Experiment around.
Buffalo chips and corn cobs were used over much of the
Great Plains and Southeast. The main thing is to use
stuff that smokes profusely rather than just burns, and
that has a pleasant aroma. Have at least a gunny sack's
worth of smoking material on hand for each couple skins
you intend to smoke.

Remember, you want smoke, not heat. When I use rotten wood, I prefer it to be slightly damp. I believe
damp smoke saturates the skin better than dry smoke.
Green boughs or leaves are already plenty damp. After
smoking, I handstretch the skin and/or pull it vigorously through a rope or wire loop to dry and buff it (this
is not a long, time-consuming operation).

To insure that I only smoke a hide (not burn it up!),
I like to position the skin a ways from the actual fire.
To do this, I have an old metal garbage can with most of
the bottom rusted and punched out that I turn upside down
over the fire pit. In the past I have used various
pipes, cans and sections of hollow logs, but I always try
to put some distance between the fire and the skin. Using an old wood stove or heater (set up outside) and a
couple sections of clean stove pipe is an excellent
smoking set-up. The draft is more easily controlled too.

In preparation for smoking, I fold a single hide in
half (along neck to tail line) and sew it into a bag
(big stitches, one half to one inch apart) from top of
neck to tips of rear legs. The bottom remains open.
With more hides to smoke, I sew two similar-sized skins
together into a bigger bag, also left open across most
of the bottom. While I don't always do this, it is well
worth the time to also sew a burlap or cloth "skirt"
(old sheets are good) around the bottom of the hide(s).
This skirt, hanging down a foot or two, is easily draped
and pinned or bound around the bottom rim of the upside
down garbage can, and further raises the skins from the
fire. The skirt arrangement lets the bottoms of the
skins smoke more evenly. Normally, the bottoms of the
skins are somewhat irregular and hard to evenly position
and seal around the can rim--portions that hang down too
far don't get smoked. If you are too lazy to sew up skin

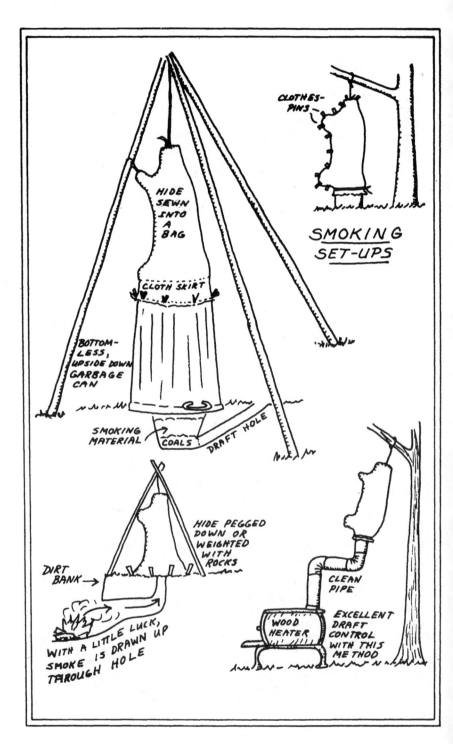

CLOTHES-PINS

SMOKING SET-UPS

HIDE SEWN INTO A BAG

CLOTH SKIRT

BOTTOM-LESS, UPSIDE DOWN GARBAGE CAN

SMOKING MATERIAL — COALS — DRAFT HOLE

HIDE PEGGED DOWN OR WEIGHTED WITH ROCKS

DIRT BANK →

WITH A LITTLE LUCK, SMOKE IS DRAWN UP THROUGH HOLE

CLEAN PIPE

WOOD HEATER

EXCELLENT DRAFT CONTROL WITH THIS METHOD

bags with cloth skirts, use clothespins, paper clips, partially-split green twigs, etc. I suppose you could even use staples.

Since the skin is to be smoked on both sides, a sewn bag is more efficiently and quickly turned inside out (without losing much good smoke) than one you must take apart, reverse and pin back together. I usually smoke the hair side of a skin first (I sew it inside out), because the first smoke is often the most billowy and thick, and permeates the skin more quickly and evenly.

Over my smoking pit I have a pole tripod set up with a rope hanging down from its center. I tie or clip this to the neck of the hide bag and adjust it for height so the cloth skirt or bottom of the hide just overlaps the can rim where I clothespin or tie it in place. The skin bag should be open inside so smoke can freely reach all parts of it. If sides of the bag tend to cling together, I prop them apart with small sticks. Often I stretch out leg sections with a piece of twine and tie them thus extended to one of the tripod poles. The poles can also be adjusted to eliminate sag in the bag. Many books will tell you to drape your hides over a tripod or dome of poles--Don't! Unless you rearrange the skins every couple minutes, they will exhibit a strange pattern of unsmoked lines wherever they were in contact with the poles.

Immediately before fastening the bag over the can, I drop a healthy amount (several handfuls) of rotton wood or boughs onto the fire (now mostly coals), then make sure everything is lined up, tight and ready to smoke away. Green juniper boughs are very pitchy and have a tendency to smoke beautifully, then suddenly burst into flame, so must be watched carefully. Rotten wood, especially if damp, takes longer to finally combust, but any smoking material should be tended carefully. Often you can anticipate a flare-up by listening to the fire. The trickiest part of smoking is keeping the fire going sufficiently to produce good, thick smoke without it getting out of hand and trying to consume everything. After all the time and energy you have invested in your buckskin to this point, don't dumbly wander off, become distracted and return to find your buckskins ablaze! I have not yet lost a whole hide (fingers crossed), but I have allowed the bottoms of a few to become badly scorched. Light scorching can be sanded off after smoking.

At any time during smoking, you should be able to hold your hand indefinitely in the smoke where it first reaches the skin. Reach your hand in and test this often. If it gets too hot for your hand, it is too hot for the buckskin. Plug the draft hole, add more smoking

Preparing to smoke a large buckskin.

material, stir up the fire a little, etc. If it does
not cool down, pour a little water on it. Always be ready to instantly pull the skin away from the fire if necessary.

If possible, avoid smoking hides on a windy day.
The wind can raise havoc with your fire control efforts,
blow the skin around and cause it to smoke unevenly.
While smoking, I plug any holes in the hide with white
cloth or toilet paper wads. These cut out some drafts,
help to hold the smoke inside and can be easily removed
to check the inside color.

I prefer to smoke my hides dark. They will fade
from sun, wear and washing soon enough, but you can keep
checking the color and stop when it pleases you. To insure complete smoke penetration, I smoke the first side
until the color is obviously soaking through most of the
skin. It will show through first, of course, in the
thinner areas. When the inside is the color I want, and
some color is generally showing through on the outside,
I turn the skin inside out and continue smoking until
done. With fairly consistent smoke, the flesh side of
the skin does not need to be smoked as long.

Smoking can take as few as ten minutes per side with
a good smoking fire, but I normally spend thirty to sixty minutes to do a whole hide (I have ended up spending a
whole lot longer with less than satisfactory smoking set-
ups). Once the hide is smoked to your satisfaction, take
it down, roll it up and put it in a bag for at least
overnight to "set" the smoke. This is not imperative,
but I think a good idea. I do it. After a night sealed
in a bag, the skin should be opened up and worked and
buffed by hand (some people lightly sand it too),
stretched by two or more people or pulled briskly through
the rope or wire loop to dissipate any moisture left from
smoking and to give it a final fluffing. I then hang it
in the sunshine and fresh air to let some of the pungent-
ly strong aroma mellow.

Once smoked, the sky and your imagination are the
only limits to what you can do with your very first buckskin. The first thing I did was to show it to everyone
I knew who I thought might be interested, and alot of
folks who weren't, too!

Remember, my descriptions here are only guidelines,
ideas, some of the methods I and others have used. There
are undoubtedly many ways you can improve on smoking arrangements, and other parts of the entire process as
well.

I see you standing there, holding your first buckskin. Do you feel you have really accomplished something? You should!

Smoking a single buckskin sewed into a bag.

Smoking 2 buckskins clothespinned together.

SOME NOTES ON THE WET-SCRAPE PROCESS

I have mentioned, alluded to and partially described the wet-scrape process for producing buckskin several times in this booklet. The purpose of this additional section is to briefly relate a few of my own experiences with this method, and with pulling hides dry and soft by hand, without using a frame. These are not instructions, only personal accounts.

Several summers ago I was conducting a short aboriginal skills workshop at a tipi camp for children on the Umatilla reservation. One of our projects was the tanning of an elk hide by the dry-scrape process. While the kids were "scratching around" on the stretched hide with the scrapers, an older Umatilla woman wandered by while gathering firewood. She watched for a little while, then sadly shook her head said "That's not the way we do it." Later, she said that she used to tan quite a bit. She first soaked a hide in the river for several days, then put it over a smoothed cottonwood log and fleshed, dehaired and grained it with a drawknife (she indicated pushing rather than pulling motions). She then brained it (I didn't get the details) and pulled the skin dry and soft entirely by hand. If intended for moccasins or everyday wear, it was smoked, using cottonwood. She said she no longer tanned because the river flooded one year and washed away her tools. Her account is essentially the same as that recorded in literally hundreds of ethnographies and other papers describing native American cultures and industries gathered during the early reservation days. What they say is true; they just don't give enough specifics for one to successfully duplicate the process.

One time a friend came by with a small, very dried deer skin she said she had begun to brain tan a couple years before, but had never completed because she could find no workable, sequential process recorded anywhere to follow. She swore that she had taken it through fleshing and graining. In its dried and contorted condition, I couldn't discern much, so we decided to carry it the rest of the way through the process as an experiment. She said she had previously soaked the skin in water until the hair slipped fairly easily, then, with a sharpened spoon, had fleshed it and scraped off the hair and grain over the round-surfaced arm of a wooden chair. Afterwards, not knowing how to proceed, she had

just let it dry. When we soaked it up, I could see that
it was well-fleshed--only some membrane remained--but
that the grain was still there. She had carefully
scraped away the dark outer layer of the epidermis, but
the main grain layer had stayed on the skin. Since it
was a small hide, we left the grain layer on and soaked
the skin in the brain slurry overnight. The next day we
thoroughly wrung it out by my standard method, then elec-
ted to pull it dry by hand. We sat facing each other on
the floor, legs outstretched, our feet planted sole to
sole firmly against each other's. Each holding an opposite margin of the skin, we leaned back to stretch it,
then on the rebound changed grips to a new spot and
leaned back again. Thus, each time we leaned back we
were stretching a different part of the skin. As the
skin began to dry and soften, we picked and peeled off
remaining membrane with our fingers and individually
pulled and stretched small, slightly stiff areas. After
three hours of nearly continuous manipulation, the skin
was soft and fluffy on the flesh side. The grain side
was also supple, but retained the slick, semi-shiny surface usually seen on chemically tanned skins. Also, we
learned that the dermal layer stretches more during softening than the less-elastic grain layer can accommodate.
As the skin was pulled and stretched, the grain layer
split and cracked open in many places, exposing the dermal layer beneath it. Although the grain was soft
enough, the cracks and splits made it appear somewhat
"ratty." When smoked, the grain surface was non-absorb-
ent; the pitchy resins accumulated on the surface, but
did not penetrate, so we smoked the fuzzy flesh side
longer.
     It is much more difficult to thoroughly soften a
larger deer hide with the grain still on because the
grain is so much thicker and less pliable, but a softened, then heavily-smoked and perhaps oiled grain surface would definitely shed rain better than fuzzy-surfaced buckskin. Small furs, obviously with both hair
and grain remaining, can be worked soft by pulling; deer
hides are generally not best tanned with the hair on.
Deer are considered "hollow-haired" animals--the hair is
brittle and, even if you can keep it from slipping during the tanning process, it will continually shed and
break off with use (as a rug, robe, etc.). The above-
described hand-softening of a small deer hide with the
grain left on does not really exemplify the wet-scrape
process in which most of the grain is removed.
     While taking most of our hides through the dry-
scrape process at Wallowa Mountain field station in the
summer of 1979, we decided to do one wet-scrape. A me-
dium-sized, already fleshed and dried deer hide was left

to soak, weighted down with big rocks, in a standard metal garbage can full of water with the lid on for most
of five days. The can sat in direct sun about half of
each day. Obviously, after five days of soaking in
slightly warm water, this was not a particularly pleasant hide to be around! The hide was removed from the
water, placed over a waist beam and quickly and easily
dehaired with the metal bar flesher. Except for a few
small spots, the hair slipped off readily. The skin was
then turned and the flesh side gone over with the flesher to remove the membrane. This was done very systematically, thoroughly and effectively, since we planned to
pull this hide dry by hand. I figured it would be harder to remove membrane later, without the hide stretched
in a frame. After membraning, the skin was again turned
over on the beam, grain side up, and the grain removed
with a very sharp drawknife. The prolonged soaking in
water had softened and swelled the grain considerably,
and over much of the hide it was fairly easily sheared
off with pushing strokes of the drawknife. Controlled
forceful pressure (which had to be learned through trial
and error) was required, however, and several cuts were
made in the skin, especially the thinner areas and spots
where the grain was tougher. On the neck and some of
the lower leg areas the grain did not want to come off
at all, so was left on for experimentation. The dehairing, membraning and wet-scraping took three or four
hours.

With most of the moisture squeegeed from the skin
from these steps, the holes were sewed closed and the
hide was then manipulated, pulled, stretched and sloshed
in the brain mixture (as previously described) for twenty minutes to half an hour, then removed and thoroughly
wrung out. For the next approximately four hours the
skin was nearly continuously worked by two methods. Initially, several people stood in a circle and pulled the
hide. It was also pulled vigorously and relentlessly
through a heavy (quarter inch diameter) wire loop affixed at two different points to a tree. When one person "burned out," another took his place. These two
methods were alternated until everyone was exasperated
and, fortunately, the hide was dry. At one point, for
variety, with several people holding the edges, we even
put a person in the center of the hide and tossed her
into the air (this was effective, but didn't last long
because laughing people have difficulty maintaining
strong grips!).

This hide turned out exceptionally soft, springy
and thick, even the areas where the grain was left on,
but it also shrunk considerably and had the characteristic paunchy center with overstretched margins of a hand-

pulled buckskin. After smoking, I made a pair of moccasins from a thick rump portion of the skin, only to have the toe areas twist so horrendously sideways after one day's wear that I was walking on the seams. This hide seemed to have rebounded and shrunk so much that pattern pieces cut from it would not retain their planned shape. The hide would have been better made into something not adversely affected by its propensity for uncontrolled stretching and twisting. While I consider this to be a successfully done wet-scraped, hand-softened buckskin, I still prefer the finished outer surface, ability to lie flat and less tendency toward extreme stretching characteristic of dry-scraped, frame-softened buckskins.

Perhaps the foregoing notes and observations will be useful should you experiment with wet-scraping and/or hand-softening.

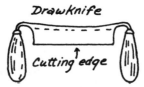

Drawknife

Cutting edge

Pulling a wet-scraped hide dry & soft through a heavy wire loop.

BUCKSKIN CLOTHING

When I began brain tanning, I wished for a book that would clearly outline the procedures I should follow. Eventually, after years of trial, error and experimentation, I ended up writing that nonexistent book I had wished for. You are now reading it!

Since I first tanned enough skins to make a shirt, I have wished for a comprehensive book that would tell me everything I ever wanted to know about making buckskin clothing. I couldn't find one, and I am beginning to feel that, with alot of additional research and experimentation, I shall have to write that book too! I'm sorry to say, this is not it, but until such time I or someone else accomplishes it, I'll briefly set down some of my ideas, observations and things I've learned along the way. I consider myself only a novice clothesmaker.

As with the various brain tanning procedures, bits and pieces of useful information on buckskin clothing, patterns, styles, sewing methods, etc., are scattered through a wide variety of sources--ethnographies and other anthropological and archaeological publications, craft, outdoor, survival and sewing books, museums, historical societies, libraries, even the stylish pattern catalogues at your local fabric shop! But I've found no single source containing all the information a "buckskin person" would want.

THE NATURE OF BUCKSKIN

So, you have tanned one or more skins and now you are anxious to MAKE something from them! One of the hardest psychological situations you will have to conquer (ah, come on--it can't be that bad!) is the moment you sit poised, scissors, knife or sharp obsidian flake in hand, waiting for some internal impulse that will cause that hand to cut into your very first buckskin (I put all that work into it, I don't want to blow it)! Hopefully, the following notes will lessen the trauma you experience and give you a more solid place to begin.

Nobody says you have to conform to any past or present standards in the type and style of clothing you make and wear. You (and the deer) created the buckskin--now, create a way to wear it! As you plan your first garments, keep in mind the nature of the material with which you will be working. Buckskin is not uniform. It varies tremendously in thickness and stretchability within the same hide and from one hide to another. It has flaws, both yours and the deer's, but they are integral to it. If "perfect" buckskin could be produced with computer-like accuracy, I likely wouldn't deal with it.

Buckskin lends itself best to free-form, loose-fitting garments that have room to stretch or shrink without appreciably altering the shape or fit. In my opinion, the less cutting and tailoring involved, the better.

Besides being the most comfortable clothing you can wear, buckskin is such a unique material that you should pattern your garments so that the best qualities of the buckskin are preserved and displayed. I would rather see skins that happened to be fashioned into uniquely personalized clothing than highly tailored, stylized clothing that happened to be made of buckskin.

Improvisation is stimulated when, due to your lack of unlimited, finished buckskins, oddly shaped skins, presence of holes, etc., you can't simply lay out and trace around prestyled pattern pieces, then assemble them. Prewhite contact native Americans did not use tape measures or precut patterns! Skins were fitted around a person or mostly "eyeballed" to determine shape, size and fit of garments. This simplicity is deceptive, however, because accurate workmanship requires a thorough understanding of the nature and qualities of buckskin and the form and movement of the human body, both of which grow with experience.

Museum collections and old photos are excellent sources for studying aboriginal buckskin clothing. Most museums that have clothing have more in storage than is on display and quite often will allow you to examine it all firsthand. Many native garments begin with whole skins and what tailoring is involved encompasses only how best to functionally fit those skins around the body. The essense of the skin, even the animal from which it came, is nearly always at the forefront when you "flash" on native apparel. Thus, each legging is basically one skin wrapped around the leg and tied or sewed to fit. Dresses and shirts are basically a whole hide in front and back with various styles of yokes and sleeves sometimes added. Loose ends, irregular margins, etc., are left as is or fringed, but seldom cut off. The resulting garments, upon critical evaluation by the "modern American straightline mentality," are asymmetrical--almost "childish" in form and design--yet in total effect are well composed, natural and beautiful. A deer wouldn't look quite right with all his legs chopped off; neither does a buckskin!

Well, so much for the ideology. All native clothing

did not adhere to this description, and most of my
clothing so far has been made from pieces cut from skins
and assembled in order to best distribute my "on hand"
(there's never enough) supply of buckskin...(Can I get
two sleeves out of that one hide? Oh yeah, just barely,
and then I can use this piece of leg for a pocket,
and....!).

WORKING WITH BUCKSKIN

Buckskin should be worn on your body as much as possible the same way the deer wore it, the hair side outside and the neck end uppermost. It just seems to hang
better this way (although some standardized Plains dress
styles were made with the rump ends up).
Try to cut like parts of a garment from like parts
of skin of approximately the same thickness and stretchability. Also, cut like pieces running in the same direction on skins. For example, two sleeve or moccasin
patterns should be laid out either both positioned
crossways or both positioned lengthways on a skin, not
one crossways and the other lengthways. This plan still
does not assure that each will stretch, shrink or adjust
to your body the same as the other, but it helps. Always avoid cutting pattern pieces from a skin on a bias
(diagonally), as they will most assuredly twist and
stretch unevenly.
A friend made a shirt once and, after a year or so
of wear, one sleeve had lengthened by about six inches
and the other had shrunk about the same, so to remedy
the situation he cut off a portion of the long one and
sewed it onto the shorter one! It has been my experience that most of my frame-worked buckskin gradually
shrinks up through years of use, wear and washings--
sleeves and pantlegs shorten, but correspondingly increase in girth. I also notice that they relengthen after washing, but only temporarily. I have added extensions to the sleeves of my first shirt (after eight
years) and to the legs of my pants (after three years).
Since the skins these garments were made from were done
several years ago, it may be that I stretched them too
tightly in the frame while working them dry, and they
are simply returning to their proper size. Just in case,
I now cut shirt and coat sleeves and pantlegs longer to
begin with. Hand-softened skins and any skins cut on a
bias tend to stretch with use. Your experiences may
vary, but the overall variability and unpredictability
of buckskin makes looser-fitting garments more practical
and versatile.
Your first buckskins are more likely to have some

holes and mended places. As you fashion garments, you can often position those spots in inconspicuous or hidden areas (bottom of sleeve, hidden by fringe, underneath pockets, beadwork, etc.). Often I have considered mended rips to be unique decorations and not worried about their placement. You may feel that the "battle scars" put on your buckskin by the deer, the hunter and you during tanning detract from a finished garment; I assure you, these flaws are the last thing noticed by others, and unless their placement structurally weakens the garment, I believe they enhance the authenticity of your handcrafted apparel.

Clothing commonly made of buckskin includes moccasins, leggings, breechcloths, pants, shirts, dresses, capes, shawls, hoods, caps, vests and coats. It is also used for bags, quivers, cradleboard covers, drum and shield covers, blankets, etc., or almost anything made nowadays of cloth, wool, synthetic fabrics and leathers. It is not within the scope of this booklet nor my present knowledge to thoroughly cover the making of all these articles, but I shall elaborate on much of the methodology and specific techniques (as I have learned them) involved in their manufacture. Of the garments, shirts will receive the most attention because they seem to be the preferred "first major garment" everyone wants to make with his buckskin. I hope the experienced tailors reading this will forgive me for all I've left out (or haven't learned yet) and for many of the terms I've "invented" to describe various styles and techniques.

METHODOLOGY OF MANUFACTURE

I have encountered three basic approaches to making buckskin clothing, although there is some overlap and the making of one garment could involve aspects of all three. The first I have termed the "free form" method. In it, whole skins, or at least large expanses of skin, are fitted to the body and only trimmed or cut enough to make the garment wearable. This involves inventorying the size, thickness and number of available buckskins, forming a general idea of what you want the garment to be like, then fitting the skins together on your body and perhaps temporarily pinning them to each other—kind of figuring and improvising as you jump right into the actual construction. Make as few cuts as possible until you can clearly see how the skins are fitting your body and fitting together. For example, the common "three skin" dress or shirt consists of one skin folded in half lengthways (along neck to tail line) to form the yoke, the top of the garment, with a second and third

skin attached to it to form the front and back. The
yoke is a piece that fits around the neck and drapes over
the shoulders slightly down the front and back, much like
a small cape. The rest of the garment is attached to,
and hangs from, the yoke. Your first actual cuts would
be two intersecting slits in a T-shape, made long enough
to just poke your head through in the approximate center
of the yoke skin. The stem of the "T" goes in front.
You would then put on the yoke hide and see how it wanted to hang, stretch, etc., before you positioned and
pinned the front and back skins in place or further enlarged or shaped the neck hole. The front and rear
skins are normally affixed to the yoke about midway between the tops of your shoulders and your nipples (and
comparably in back), thus the yoke skin overlaps these
pieces and hangs down considerably. All or part of the
yoke skin below the front and back seams is usually later
fringed. With front and back skins attached, you would
next determine the position of the side seams or ties
(joining front and back skins) with respect to your torso
size and free body and arm movement. The portions of
front and back hides that extend beyond the side seams
would also later be fringed. At this point you would
have a basic tunic-like garment fitted to your body that
is crude, but functional as is or open to further refinements and/or embellishments (as fringing the bottom, adding longer sleeves, refining neck hole, etc.). With a
whole skin in both front and back, this garment is usually about knee length. If you prefer it not to be this
long, use only half skins for the front and back panels.
    You can make a yokeless free form shirt or dress by
beginning with only two skins joined across their shoulder areas to fit over your shoulders, leaving a neck
slit in the center, then, with the garment on, determining placement of the side seams or ties as above. Should
you have only a single, large buckskin, you can still
make a one-piece shirt. Fold the hide in half across the
middle of the back (not lengthways) so that neck and rump
ends are about even with each other. Cut the T-shaped
neck opening along the center of the fold, put the skin
on and determine placement of side and underarm seams or
ties. All four leg portions of the skin can then be cut
off and pieced together to lengthen the sleeves. This
simple style is basically making an entire (though usually shorter) shirt from a large yoke.
    Free form variations are endless and provide you with
semi-fitted clothing without relying on predetermined
pattern pieces. No matter what style of garment you make,
the basic tenets of the free form method are adapting, adjusting, figuring and fitting as you create and construct
the garment. Some people are much better at free forming

than others.

Clothing, usually torso coverings, produced by the second major approach or method of manufacture (as practiced by native Americans) has been termed "binary" clothing by the Denver Art Museum. Binary means anything made or existing in two sections, usually a front and back, and while it does not wholly describe examples in this category, is an adequate generic term. Many garments produced by the free form method are binary in composition, but differ in that they are more or less fitted to the body as they are made. Binary garments, as defined here, are not fitted. They employ simple, often geometric shapes and straight-line seams, and "fit" only because they are made large enough. In a binary shirt, for example, front and back are usually of equal size and shape and are joined at the shoulders and sides with straight-line seams or ties. Sleeves are basically rectangular pieces of skin folded in half and affixed to the tunic portion in straight seams. They usually extend straight out from the sides of the tunic as a continuation of the shoulder line.

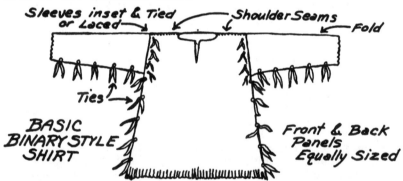

A binary shirt, especially if made too small, tends to not feel "quite right" around the neck and shoulders and to constrict and inhibit free arm movement in the shoulder and sleeve seam areas. In the free form and prefitted pattern methods, the back of a shirt is wider than the front, just as your body is shaped. Likewise, in the prefitted pattern method (to be described below), both the sleeves and tunic are shaped where they join to allow freer, more natural arm movement. Native seamstresses probably just eyeballed the sizes, shapes and lengths of binary shirt pieces (the ends and bottoms of sleeves and sides and bottoms of the tunic were not always trimmed to geometric shapes) for any given person, assembled the pieces and came as close to a correct fit as is possible with this style of garment. Fortunately,

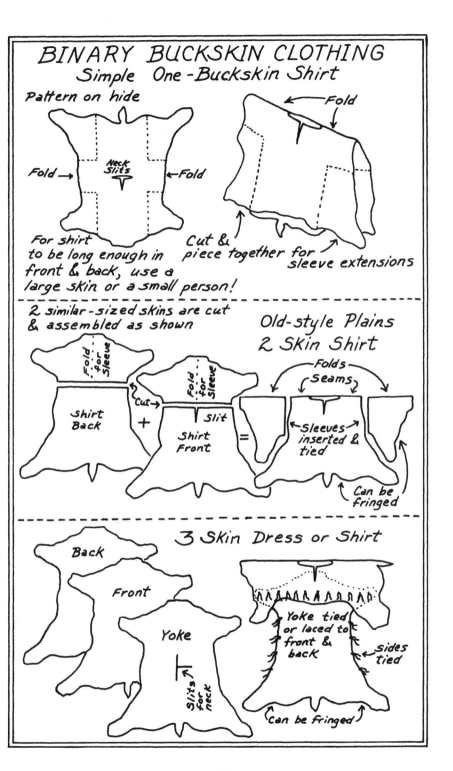

BINARY BUCKSKIN CLOTHING
Simple One-Buckskin Shirt

Pattern on hide

Fold →   ←Fold

Neck Slits

←Fold   ←Fold

For shirt to be long enough in front & back, use a large skin or a small person!

Cut & piece together for sleeve extensions

2 similar-sized skins are cut & assembled as shown

Fold for Sleeve

Shirt Back

Cut→

+

Fold for Sleeve

Slit

Shirt Front

=

Old-style Plains 2 Skin Shirt

Folds

Seams

←Sleeves inserted & tied

Can be fringed

3 Skin Dress or Shirt

Back

Front

Yoke

Slits for neck

Yoke tied or laced to front & back

Sides tied

Can be fringed

due to the nature of buckskin, binary garments eventually adjust and conform pretty well to the body shape and movements of the wearer. You can eyeball the pieces, or lay out a __roomy__ old cloth shirt or dress to use as a general guide to getting the dimensions of adequate size. You can make a binary shirt or dress much easier and faster than by the other methods described here, but remember, in the initial phase of wear its fit will take some getting used to while it adjusts. Various neck reinforcements, closures, collars, cuffs, pockets, etc., can be added however you wish.

The third major method in the construction of buckskin clothing begins with a preconceived, preset and precut series of pattern forms laid out and positioned most advantageously (following the previously described guidelines, if possible) on your available buckskins. The skins are then cut out to the pattern shapes and the process of assembling them begins.

MAKING YOUR OWN PATTERNS

If you are leary of "jumping into" the open-endedness of constructing a free form garment, you want something better fitted than the binary style and you can find no predesigned pattern that turns you on, you will have to make your own. My clothing is mostly a combination of homemade or altered patterns and free form adaptations. It has been my experience that no buckskin garment is created by simply cutting out the various pattern pieces to their prescribed shapes and sizes and assembling them-- unforseen problems always crop up and call for some ingenuity and improvisation! A common problem faced by those of us who are not experienced seamsters or seamstresses is learning that pattern pieces (especially sleeves and yokes), when laid out flat, are shaped much differently than one would guess while looking at a finished garment. It is usually the strangeness of the shape that makes the piece fit correctly to the rest of the garment and to your body! Getting a well-fitting, workable pattern figured out is for me the hardest part of making buckskin clothing, and unless you are experienced, I suggest keeping them as simple and basic as possible (they'll seem entirely too complex anyway by the time you are done!).

The easiest way to make your own pattern is to find an old cloth garment (shirt, vest, coat, dress, pants-- whatever you intend to make) that __fits you loosely and comfortably__ and carefully cut it apart to form the basis of your buckskin pattern. If you really don't want to cut apart your favorite old shirt, try to pick up a similar one cheaply at garage or rummage sales, the Goodwill or Salvation Army thrift stores, etc. Most commercial clothing, however, consists of more and smaller pattern pieces sewed together than are necessary or desirable on comparable buckskin garments, so try to simplify them if possible. Don't immediately cut a shirt apart along all seams, but notice if you can leave some seams as they are and still have the pattern pieces lie flat. The fewer seams the better in your buckskin clothing. Smaller pattern pieces in key places (especially the yoke area), should they stretch unevenly, are more likely to throw the whole garment askew. You will seldom find a cloth shirt that is constructed exactly the way you would want a buckskin shirt, so before cutting, you must determine if the style of buckskin shirt you want can be made by modifying the cloth shirt you have. While buckskin shirt styles have already been partially described, let's take another look at them in in reference to making patterns.

There are two general styles of buckskin shirts--those with yokes and those without. Good patterns for both can be made from cloth shirts. The yoked shirt, in its simplest form, consists of the yoke, a front and a back and two sleeves--ideally, only five different large pieces of buckskin. The yokeless shirt, in its simplest form, consists of only four main pieces--the front and back (joined by seams at the shoulders) and two sleeves. A yoked shirt allows you to have fringe across both the upper front and back of the shirt; the simpler four piece yokeless shirt does not, but can be modified. You can design a "hybrid" or "compositely-yoked" shirt in this same style (with shoulder seams)by making both the front and the back in two pieces--a smaller upper piece and a larger lower piece. The upper piece overlaps the lower piece; the amount of overlap will be the length of the fringe. In other words, when the two upper pieces are joined by the shoulder seams, they become a yoke, and they can thus be fringed along their bottom edges. This modified style is handy if you don't have skins long enough to form complete, one-piece fronts and backs. There are many other workable shirt styles than I am discussing here; if you find another one that pleases you more, go for it!

Many cloth shirts, no matter how they were constructed, can be cut apart at different places (not along existing seams) to make patterns for the just described buckskin shirts. Based on my experiences, I believe the greatest potential problem you will face in designing a fully yoked shirt is in the area at the tops of the sleeves, where they join the yoke. On a buckskin shirt, a full yoke normally hangs over the ends of your shoulders and part way down your upper arms. This means that

101

the tops of the sleeves are attached to the yoke a couple inches below your arm-shoulder joint, that the yoke actually functions as the upper couple inches of the sleeves and that the sleeves are thus shorter than they would be on a shirt with seams placed right at the arm-shoulder joints. Now, cloth shirts are simply not constructed this way, so to cut a full yoke pattern, you must include the tops of the sleeves with the yoke. If you become somewhat frustrated (as I do) first trying to figure out a workable yoke pattern and later trying to smoothly attach sleeves, front and back pieces to the yoke, you can always lighten things up a bit with a few yoke jokes! Full, fringed yokes on buckskin shirts are beautiful--I just always feel like I've been through hell by the time I get one completed to my satisfaction. Yokeless or compositely-yoked shirts have their little quirks of construction too, but are considerably easier to figure out.

Once you have determined the style of shirt you intend to make, cut apart the cloth shirt according to your projections and see if it will work for your pattern. If not, get another old shirt and try again! If so, you should make paper or cardboard patterns from the cut-apart shirt pieces (by the way, it helps considerably to iron a cloth shirt before you cut it apart). As you transfer the cloth pieces to paper, remember to incorporate blocks of space that will become fringe, any other necessary alterations you have decided upon and be sure to allow an extra third to half inch on all edges that will be part of seams. Paper or cardboard pattern pieces are much easier to work with than the cloth shirt pieces because they better maintain their shape, are more efficiently arranged and switched around on your buckskins and are easier to trace around when you've got them all laid out just right.

To digress briefly, this step (paper patterns) may be less important for pants construction. To make my buckskin pants, I just cut apart an old pair of jeans and laid the material right on the buckskins (both front panels on one hide and both backs on another), then traced around them with a pencil. The only alterations I made were on the front panels, which I cut several inches wider than the jeans legs. With the jeans legs laid out lengthways on the hide, there was about five inches of buckskin showing between the outside seams of the jeans and the side margins of the hide, so I just left this on. This extra more or less five inch strip running the entire length from waist to cuff along the outside of each leg was cut as fringe once the pants were assembled. I also, by eyeballing, doubled the width of the fly "flap" on each panel so it could be doubled back

102

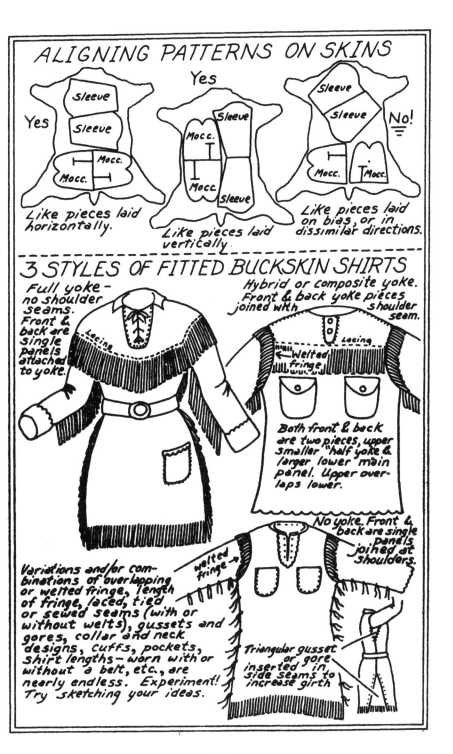

ALIGNING PATTERNS ON SKINS

Yes

Sleeve
Sleeve
Mocc.
Mocc.

Like pieces laid horizontally.

Yes

Mocc.
Sleeve
Mocc.
Sleeve

Like pieces laid vertically.

Sleeve
Sleeve
Mocc.
Mocc.

No!

Like pieces laid on bias, or in dissimilar directions.

3 STYLES OF FITTED BUCKSKIN SHIRTS

Full yoke - no shoulder seams. Front & back are single panels attached to yoke.

Lacing

Hybrid or composite yoke. Front & back yoke pieces joined with shoulder seam.

Lacing

←Welted fringe

Both front & back are two pieces, upper smaller "half yoke" & larger lower main panel. Upper over-laps lower.

No yoke. Front & back are single panels joined at shoulders.

Welted fringe →

Variations and/or combinations of overlapping or welted fringe, length of fringe, laced, tied or sewed seams (with or without welts), gussets and gores, collar and neck designs, cuffs, pockets, shirt lengths — worn with or without a belt, etc., are nearly endless. Experiment! Try sketching your ideas.

Triangular gusset or gore inserted in side seams to increase girth

on itself--the double thickness making a stronger, heavier base for sewing on antler buttons to one flap and for cutting buttonholes less apt to stretch out of shape in the other. I also made the waistband double thickness. And now, back to paper patterns!

When laid out on your buckskin, the paper patterns should be pinned in place or weighted down so the buckskin doesn't "crawl" as you trace around the patterns with a soft-leaded pencil. Pencil will eventually wear off; don't use marker pens or ballpoints. I usually lay my pattern pieces on the flesh sides so any markings will be hidden anyway when the garment is finished. Before you do any tracing or cutting, MAKE SURE THE PATTERN PIECES ARE LAID OUT CORRECTLY IN RELATION TO EACH OTHER AS THEY WILL BE FITTED TOGETHER!!! You don't want to end up cutting out two right sleeves (and thus one wrong one!). Visualize the whole garment assembled from the pieces as you have them laid out. Make sure the pattern pieces are aligned correctly on the skins (as previously described), like pieces running the same direction, etc. After you feel you have everything laid out correctly, check through it all one more time, then cut the pieces out!

What I usually do at this stage, especially with a shirt, is pin the whole thing together and very carefully crawl into it. Of course, it is not quite the same fit when only pinned together and it looks pretty strange with all those as yet uncut fringe flaps sticking out, but I can usually assess the success so far. If you do this, try not to unduly stretch any of the freshly cut edges.

The order in which you actually lace or sew a garment together is largely up to you, but I prefer to begin at the top--shoulder seams or yoke--and kind of work down. I always do sleeves last. Sometimes, once you complete the shoulder seams on a yokeless shirt or get the front and back panels affixed to the yoke and try the thing on again, you'll find that it wants to ride or hang a little differently than you had planned. Most commonly, this involves a general tendency to pull to the rear or to the front. Temporarily pin the sides closed again and see if this helps. You may have to slightly alter the shape and/or position of the neck hole, or readjust and repin the sides until you get it to ride right.

Some basic lacing and sewing techniques will be covered shortly, but first I want to elaborate on fringe.

FRINGE

Let's face it, long fringe is beautiful! It gently blows in the wind, ripples and flows as you walk and adds

104

an element of grace to your every movement. Long fringe makes a simple buckskin shirt a real personalized artistic creation.

But, let's face it, long fringe is about as practical for everyday wear as Charlie Brown going through the day all tangled up in his kite string! It will drag through your banana cream pie, your pot of beans or coffee, your campfire; it will collect pitch, paint, burrs, soot and miscellaneous unknown substances; it will get caught in your car door, your handsaw teeth, your can opener and your zipper; it will wrap around your gearshift, your fire drill, your bowstring and your neck while running. And these examples are just for starters!

If you make a shirt for special occasions, make the fringe as long as you want, but if you are making an everyday, working shirt, one that is designed for function, keep the fringe shorter, about two to four inches. On the sleeves, where fringe is most likely to be in your way, it shouldn't hang below the cuff as you stand, arms hanging at your sides.

Fringe has purposes other than decoration. Fringe probably began when people found that many small slits cut along the bottom edges of buckskin garments hastened drying when those garments became wet. As the water naturally drained downward through a buckskin garment as worn on the body or hung up, the original short, usually wide fringe exposed more skin surfaces to the air than a single, unfringed edge. The fringe provided a "wicking" action that actually drew the water from the main expanse of the garment and hastened evaporation. The few examples I have seen of the oldest buckskin shirts from the Great Plains have little, if any, real fringe--the bottom edges are slightly slit, scalloped or pinked. While I am partial to long, thin fringe, I believe it is less functional. It tends to dry too fast from the bottom up. Wider fringe (which I don't think looks as good) has enough body to both draw the water down into it and let it evaporate more efficiently.

All in all, the wicking action of fringe may be of negligible importance or function to your buckskin clothing, but the evolution of fringe from its meager beginnings to the incorporation of wholly fringed hides into some late nineteenth century native costumes makes an interesting study. There are many other assertions concerning the function of fringe (allows you to sneak through the woods more quietly, visually disrupts your outline, thus making you a more amorphous target in the eyes of an enemy, etc.), but at the very least, fringed clothing gives you a nearly endless supply of short buckskin thongs, should you need them out in the wilderness!

Fringe is incorporated into buckskin clothing in two

main ways, overlapping and sewing it into seams as welts.
On a shirt with a yoke, the bottom of the yoke is
fringed and overlaps the front and back panels and the
tops of the sleeves. Sleeves and pantlegs can be cut
wider than needed for proper fit and laced together with
the extra width overlapping and cut for fringe. Fringe
incorporated into a seam as a welt is described in the
next section.
　　Strips of fringe simply sewed or laced onto a shirt,
vest, coat, etc. (as commonly seen on cheaply made but
expensive to buy commercial leather garments) may look
good to drugstore buckskinners for decoration, but are
useless. You went to all the trouble to produce your
own buckskin--don't cheapen it by copying functionless
commercial styles.

LACING AND SEWING TECHNIQUES

　　I think buckskin clothing looks best when it is,
wherever practical, laced together with buckskin thongs.
Clothing can also be sewed with thinner buckskin thongs,
sinew or various heavy-duty linen, cotton or synthetic
threads. Natural plant fibers you collect and process
yourself can also be used. These are stripped from the
stems, cleaned with brisk rubbing between the hands,
then hand-twisted into two-ply string for sewing. They
include the fibers of stinging nettle, Indian hemp (dogbane), marijuana, milkweed, yucca, wild flax and others
with which I've had little or no experience. Combined
methods can also be used; the outside seams of my buckskin pants are overlapped and laced with long buckskin
thongs; the inner leg seams are welted and sewed with
dogbane fiber string, and all the patches are sewed on
with shoemaker's commercial linen cord (because I was in
a hurry)!
　　Much old native buckskin clothing was not sewed or
laced at all, but pieces were simply tied together with
buckskin thongs every few inches. The sides and sleeves
of my first buckskin shirt are only tied together. Tied
seams are great in warm weather when air circulation is
desirable, but are not exactly cozy during a blizzard.
Believing that his buckskin clothing should be versatile,
Slim used to lace the sides of his everyday buckskin
shirt closed in winter, then in warmer weather, remove
the lacing and loosely tie them in two or three spots.
The thongs used for tying can be left fairly long to appear as fringe.
　　Long thongs for lacing can be cut from a skin by following the contours where large pattern pieces were cut
out, or from smaller pieces by rounding the corners and
cutting one continuous strip in spiral fashion. Thongs

intended for lacing should be thoroughly stretched before use. They will sometimes increase in length by
half from stretching and will of course become narrower
by about half also (stretchability varies with the thickness of the skin and the part of a hide from which it was
cut). Strips should be cut almost twice as wide as you
want the lacing to be. The prestretching will make for
a tighter laced seam and will retard the edges of the
pieces being laced together from stretching out of
shape.

Holes for lacing pieces of buckskin together should
be made with a sharp awl (a modified ice pick will do).
I first align or position the pieces where I want them,
then pin them together. Use a soft (cottonwood, pine,
etc.) flat board as backing and hold the awl vertically
as you poke the holes. Holes should be made with an awl
because it does little dammage to the skin--mostly separates and compresses the fibers. After lacing, awl holes
tend to "fill back in" around the lacing, thus making a
tighter seam. Holes made with a leather punch or slits
cut with a sharp knife will gradually but continually
stretch and enlarge and make a loose, sloppy seam (I
know! I made slits to lace my first shirt together).

I place the holes about a quarter inch in from any
edges and space them regularly a quarter inch apart.
Some people prefer larger lacing and wider spacing of
holes. Slim showed me a handy little guide you can easily make for evenly spacing and straightly aligning lacing holes. Take a narrow, thin, flat, straight-side little piece of wood (a wooden ruler without the metal edge
works fine) about six inches long and mark it at quarter
inch intervals. Then, with sharp knife, small saw or
triangular file, notch it at each quarter inch mark, so
the "V" of the notch is right in line with the mark.
Smooth it up and you have a useful little gauge. The illustration is about actual size.

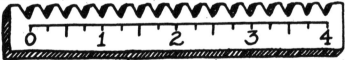

Lay it on the buckskin and either mark the spots for the
holes with pencil or just directly punch them with the
awl.

When I lace the yoke to the front or back panel of a
shirt, I usually begin in the center and lace outward to
the sides; this seems to keep the pieces aligned better
and gives these dominant seams a neater appearance. If
you start at one side and work all the way across, there
is more chance of the pieces "pulling" to one side or
the other. For running the lacing through the holes, I

107

use a large-eyed needle, usually a homemade bone or antler one, because the tip is slightly rounded and doesn't catch in the buckskin (it's also nicer to watch as you lace!).

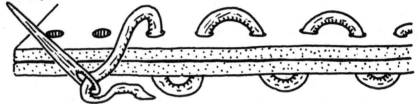

When lacing, try to keep the buckskin lace from twisting--the seam will be flatter and neater. Eventually, laced seams will loosen a bit, so draw up your stitches tight, slightly bunching the material between each stitch. When I reach the end of each laced section, I just leave the ends of the lacing loose until the entire garment is finished. Then, if need be, I tighten or adjust the lacing and knot the ends or run each one back under itself for a few stitches. This of course is done on the inside of the garment. If you tie knots and later find them digging into your skin, pound them with a rock or hammer and they'll flatten right out.

Anyplace on a finished garment where there is a raw edge of buckskin, the edge will gradually stretch. Sometimes, as the bottom of a shirt adjusting to fit around the hips, or bottom ends of sleeves, pants and leggings slightly flaring, this is desirable, but all around the margins of vests, the fronts of coats, the waistbands of pants and skirts and especially the necks of any garments, it is undesirable. To reduce stretching, poke awl holes and run a well prestretched lace all along the edges, following the same spacing and procedure as described for lacing pieces together. This functional maneuver also lends a decorative touch to the edges. There are other styles of both functional and decorative lacing you can use. Raw edges can also be hemmed, but unless done on thin buckskin, can become rather bulky.

Some seams you may decide to sew rather than lace. Seams are always sewed inside out. I use either the whip stitch (also called overhand stitch--see illustration in buckskin process section on staking hides) or the lacing stitch almost exclusively, and sometimes I combine them-- several lacing stitches, then a whip stitch back through the last lacing stitch, then several more lacing stitches, etc. For tight, neat seams, with or without a welt, I believe the lacing stitch is better. The stitches will seldom show from the outside of the seam. By either method, I cinch each stitch up tightly. For any sewing, as for lacing, holes should first be made with an awl.

Buckskin is a tough material to force a needle through, and is often unduly stretched by so-doing. For quick mending jobs where you must both make the holes and sew with a needle, a tiangular needle works best.

A welted seam is one that, instead of simply sewing two edges together, has a thin (quarter to half inch wide) buckskin strip inserted between the two edges of the garment. This strip, the welt, sandwiched between the edges, is incorporated into, and thus becomes part of the finished seam. Welted seams are bulkier, but sturdier. The welt makes the seam tighter, more durable and windproof. Welted seams are commonly used in heavy-duty moccasins, coats, mittens, gloves, etc., but refine the seams of any garment.

Instead of using only a thin strip for a welt, you can use one edge of a wider strip (as wide as your fringe is to be long). Thus, when the seam is completed (sewed inside out), most of the wide strip protrudes from the outside of the seam for the entire length of the seam. The strip is then cut to form the fringe.

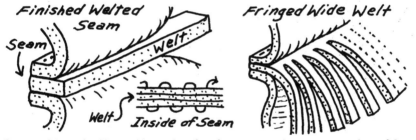

Finished Welted Seam — *Seam* — *Welt* — *Welt* — *Inside of Seam* — *Fringed Wide Welt*

The welt, whether the standard narrow type or made wider for fringe, does not have to be one continuous piece. You can trim your buckskin scraps to the desired size and lay several side by side in the seam. Fringed welts are much easier to work with if you cut the fringe after sewing the seams.

On a shirt or coat without a yoke, fringe is common-ly welted into the sleeve-to-body seams, or into the side seams of any garments that do not have overlapping fringe. Like buckskin lacing, fringe will stretch--leng-then and decrease in width--with wear and use, so take that into account when you do your cutting. I like thin fringe and usually cut about six to eight strips per inch. I've dubbed one of my shirts with absurdly long, skinny fringe my "spaghetti" shirt!

POCKETS

Aboriginal clothing seldom had pockets. I am so ac-customed to pockets that I feel a bit frustrated without

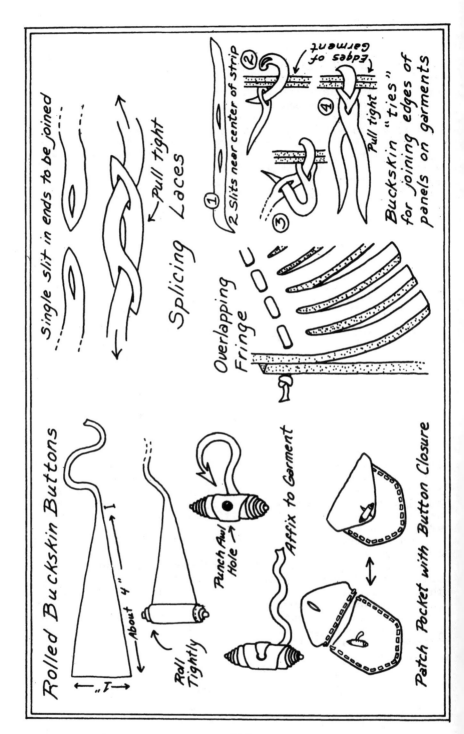

Single slit in ends to be joined

Splicing Laces

Pull tight

① 2 slits near center of strip

② ③ ④

Edges of Garment

Pull tight

Buckskin "ties" for joining edges of panels on garments

Overlapping Fringe

Rolled Buckskin Buttons

About 4"

"T"

Roll Tightly

Punch Awl Hole →

Affix to Garment

Patch Pocket with Button Closure

them. I've always hated those fads that come along every few years for pocketless shirts and pants. They say you can't take it with you, but I can carry enough selected items in my pockets to sustain me indefinitely in the wilderness. I guess that still doesn't put me at parr with those pocketless aborigines, does it? I'm working on it, but until then, I'll keep my pockets!

I've used two types of pockets on buckskin clothing--patch pockets and sack or bag pockets. The rear pockets on a pair of jeans are patch pockets and the front ones are bag pockets. Patch pockets are by far the most common and easy to make. They are simply squares or rectangles (sometimes with rounded corners or other modifications) of buckskin laced or sewed onto garments wherever pockets are desired. They are more functional if you sew on a flap above each one, with a button closure. This is especially a good idea on shirt pockets where you are otherwise apt to lose stuff when you lean over. I find patch pockets entirely adequate for most uses, although when full they tend to be rather lumpy. They can be made roomier by cutting the pocket piece larger than the area on the garment where it will sit, then "bunching" or gathering it between the stitches as you lace or sew it in place.

Sack pockets require a bit more skill in manufacturing, but are worth the effort for the front two pockets on buckskin pants and perhaps coats. They are more comfortable and hold more. The easiest way to make them is to simply sew a couple buckskin pouches patterned after the regular jeans pockets. Their main drawback is that, to set them into place, you must cut a slit through the front panels of the pants, then sew or lace each side of the top of the pocket to its corresponding side of the slit. Cutting the slits weakens the structure and support of the pants and, after you've shoved your hands in and out a few hundred times, the opening, the pocket and your pants tend to droop, sag and bag! Double-facing the edges at the opening and double-stitching the ends of the initial slit will help prevent too much distortion.

In aboriginal cultures, pouches and bags seem to have served the same function as pockets.

BUCKSKIN ODDS AND ENDS

When I first visited Slim and Sonny at their respective log cabins in the southwestern Oregon mountains, I was overwhelmed that they had so many articles of buckskin clothing, homemade bows, arrows, knives, drums and an endless parade of additional accouterments representative of primitive lifeways. After three solid days (and most

of the nights.) of storytelling, information sharing and
just plain camaraderie, things had leveled off to an understanding more than an amazement, I had learned more
about natural history, anthropology, economics, wilderness survival and human nature than my college teachers
could have ever hoped to impart and, with a notebook
full of somewhat hastily and confusingly scribbled
instructions, was on my way to producing my own buckskin.
When I finally stated one more time that I had to leave--
and meant it--I asked Slim if he had a couple small odds
and ends of buckskin that I could have to maybe make a
headband or a pouch. He disappeared into the other room,
rummaged around like a packrat seemingly endlessly, but
eventually returned to the kitchen with a giant cardboard
carton FULL of buckskin scraps! For some reason, I was
more overwhelmed than initially. "Real wealth," I thought
to myself, "is having a box of buckskin scraps...and hardly knowing where they are!"
     I made my headband, but lost it behind a dresser in a
cheapy motel room in Jackson Hole a year later, and I now
have two cartons of my own buckskin scraps--one little
piece is stapled inside the back cover of this booklet.
     Well readers, we're down to the odds and ends of this
buckskin clothing and patterns section, and I'm afraid
they are not going to be anywhere near as useful as a box
of buckskin scraps! At least, by this stage of the game,
you should be well on your way to starting your own box
of buckskin odds and ends. And perhaps another time, a-
nother place, I can truthfully tell you everything you
always wanted to know about working with buckskin. On
the other hand, maybe you can tell me!

ADDITIONAL CLOTHING AND PATTERN NOTES

     Breechcloths of buckskin, tanned furs or woven plant
fibers were the only standardized garment worn by nearly
all aboriginal American peoples. Basic breechcloth is
simply a four or five foot long (they can be much longer),
one foot wide section of buckskin worn in conjunction
with a buckskin thong tied around the waist. The breechcloth runs between the legs with each end pulled up and
under the waistband. The remainder of each free end then
hangs down, over the waistband, front and rear. In warm
weather or in warmer climates the breechcloth was often
the only garment worn. You can sometimes get a long e-
nough breechcloth from the neck to rump section of a big
hide, or you can piece one together from smaller scraps.
     Pants, as we know them, never became part of the abo-
riginal costume because they interfered with the accustomed freedom of movement that the breechcloth allowed.
Instead, in colder weather, leggings took their place.

112

Leggings are buckskin tubes or cylinders, just like individual pantlegs. One is pulled onto each leg and tied to the waist thong at each hip. I squeezed two complete leggings out of one large buckskin, but each aboriginal legging often used a whole small to medium skin--the extra skin at the side was fringed. Leggings and a breechcloth worn together still left parts of the thighs bare, so winter buckskin shirts were made long enough, nearly reaching the knees, to cover these areas.

For those accustomed to wearing pants, wearing a breechcloth and leggings may take some getting used to. Once you adjust to a breechcloth however (took me about thirty seconds!), shorts or cutoffs will never again hold any attraction (forget about the neighbors--they could probably use something more interesting to talk about than taxes and gas prices anyway)! As the day changes from cool to warm, it surely is handy to just "take your legs off" instead of going somewhere to change into cutoffs.

Buckskin moccasins give you magic feet! They are so form-fitting and comfortable, almost as if they weren't there at all, that you feel you could start running and suddenly just fly into the air. The only style I feel really familiar with is the soft-sole, wrap-top mitten moccasin. It is also sometimes called the Salish side-seam moccasin. This style was the most common in the Pacific Northwest plateau and mountain regions. I have made and worn these buckskin moccasins for about eighty per cent of the last ten years (the unaccounted for twenty per cent is because they're not so good in real wet weather if you like dry feet, but in winter I often wear them inside rubber boots or mukluks).

Any tracker knows that different people have different walking habits--some people go through a pair of buckskin moccasins in less than a week--but I usually go through the equivalent of about four to six pairs a year. I say equivalent, because most often I resole a pair more than once, and recycle the uppers several times. If this sounds like a hassle, remember that for a few days of work tanning and sewing, I have a year's worth of footwear for free! Buckskin moccasins last much longer with the good earth under your feet; asphalt and concrete are hell on them--you might as well stand around and scuff your feet on sandpaper! When I go to town, I walk on the grass whenever possible.

Construction techniques and instructions for making wrap-top mitten moccasins are illustrated.

In an earlier inventory of articles commonly made of buckskin, I neglected to include skirts, mittens and gloves. Perhaps it's just as well, as I've made only one pair of mittens, and they turned out a little tight

113

BUCKSKIN WRAP-TOP MITTEN MOCCASINS

★ Wide use in N.W. forest & plateau regions
★ Judicious use of buckskin
★ Snug, comfortable "forms to the feet" fit

① Stand barefooted or sock-footed (however you intend to wear your moccs.) on paper or cardboard and trace the outline of one foot, hold-pencil vertically as you move it snugly around the foot. Then smooth-out outline (around toes, etc.).

② I've found this moccasin to fit the foot better if you next slightly alter the shape of your foot outline (as tested by about 50 people). Don't shorten the length any, just move the longest toe-heel length to more in the center at the toe end by "chopping off" part of the big toe. For some reason this works better. If your foot is naturally shaped this way, ignore this step. Then cut out the foot.

Typical foot Outline   Altered Outline

③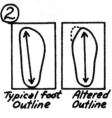

¼-⅓" for seam

Follow natural contour to here (widest part of foot behind little toe).

Fold — Heel basically centered on pattern

Imaginary line parallel with fold

Square Corner   ½-¾" between heel & edge   About 1-1½"

Lay out your altered foot pattern on a folded sheet of heavy paper or thin cardboard as shown in the diagram. The measurements are not exact, but are averages. Buckskin is adaptable. So far I've never seen anyone make moccasins from the pattern & dimensions shown, & not be satisfied with them. When you make several pairs a year, you get so you just eyeball the positioning. Trace around it & cut it out, then make a second copy. One for each foot makes positioning them on a skin easier.

④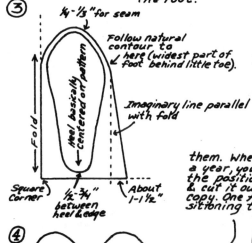

Sole Side   Vamp Side

About ←2"→

Fold

Full basic pattern for Rt. foot

Stand on the pattern. The position of the roughly 2" cross cut corresponds to the base of the steepest part of your ankle. It should be slightly closer to the rear of the pattern than to the toe, & slightly closer to the instep (fold) side than to the outside. The stem of the T-shaped cut runs from the center of the cross cut to the approx. center of the rear of the pattern (halfway from fold to outside corner). You can draw & cut these lines on the pattern, or wait & do them directly on the buckskin.

⑤ Lay both patterns on your buckskin (Thick neck skin is best for long wear), aligning them as previously described. Trace around them with pencil & cut them out. Make sure you have a right & a left foot!

⑥ Fold
Fold each buckskin piece in half (along instep fold), INSIDE OUT, & poke awl holes, positioned & spaced as previously described for shirt construction. If you are welting the seams, cut & insert the welts before you make the holes. Holes can be spaced as closely as you wish.
Begin sewing with whip or lacing stitch at the big toe side (where fold begins) and continue all the way around to the heel. Pull stitches very tight - they will receive alot of stress during wear. Since I don't cut the T-shaped slits until the next step, at the completion of this sewing, my moccasins look like thumbless mittens!

⑦ (Optional, if you have already made the T-shaped cuts). When I reach this stage, I turn the moccasins right side out, flatten & distend the seams slightly, out to shape (as with the rounded end of a broom handle shoved up inside), then place my bare foot on each one to determine the position for the cross cut. I believe this is more accurate because the side seams are already sewed. The 2" cross cut is made closer to the fold side so it will sit right on top of your foot in the finished moccasin. If initially centered, the slit moves toward the outside of your foot when you put the moccasin on and the fold side adjusts up into your arch. The tongue will be sewed to the cross cut.

⑧ Now, sew up the heel seam. With the T-shaped slit made, you can just turn the rear part of the moccasin inside out for sewing. Even-up the top corners, insert welt if desired, & make awl holes all the way down to the fold. Begin sewing at the corners & proceed to the fold at bottom.

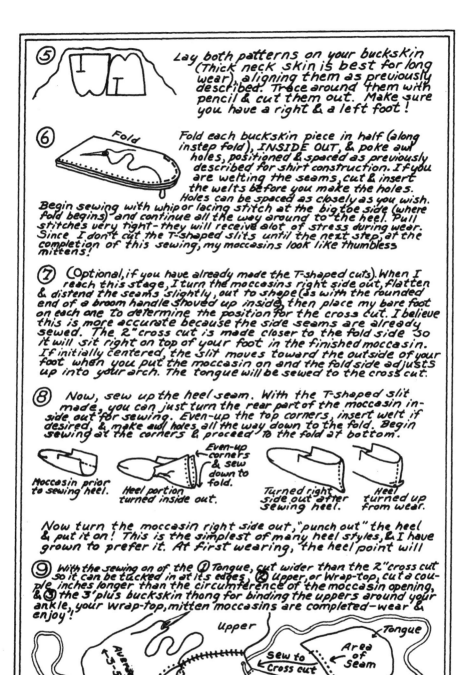

Moccasin prior to sewing heel.

Even-up corners & sew down to fold.
Heel portion turned inside out.

Turned right side out after sewing heel.

Heel turned up from wear.

Now turn the moccasin right side out, "punch out" the heel & put it on! This is the simplest of many heel styles, & I have grown to prefer it. At first wearing, the heel point will

⑨ With the sewing on of the ① Tongue, cut wider than the 2" cross cut so it can be tucked in at its edges, ② Upper, or Wrap-top, cut a couple inches longer than the circumference of the moccasin opening, & ③ the 3' plus buckskin thong for binding the uppers around your ankle, your wrap-top, mitten moccasins are completed—wear & enjoy!

Upper

Tongue

Average 5"-5½"

Sew to Cross cut

Area of Seam

Awl Holes

Buckskin wrap-top mitten moccasins. All have been sewed with welted seams.

across the butt of my palms. With a good pattern, however, mittens are fairly easy to construct. I think the best approach would be to cut apart an old mitten that fits you and use it for your pattern. Otherwise, with an untested pattern (and they're a dime a dozen in the various sources I've already mentioned) make a cloth dummy first to see if the pattern is workable. Gloves are another story, but again, the secret lies in having a good pattern. Some friends went through about two whole buckskins and six "not quite right" pairs of gloves before they proudly said, "Hey, look at these!" I have the pattern (but my fingers are longer) and I haven't tried it yet.

In this clothing and patterns section, I have not detailed many of the refinements and embellishments for buckskin clothing. Such aspects as cuffs, buttons, neck closures, collar styles, plus a million other little "unknowns" you will have to determine and figure out on your own. The next time I make a shirt or a pair of pants I know I'll encounter all sorts of things I should have included here.

Buckskin clothing should not be static; it should be versatile and free to grow and change just as you do. If you don't like something about your shirt, change it! Experiment. If your buckskin is well made from good hides, you'll have a lifetime to get it right!

CARE OF BUCKSKIN CLOTHING

Much has already been said in passing about the unique properties, quirks and care of buckskin, so this last section will just kind of round out what you should know. Basically, take care of your buckskin garments just as you would wool ones. Buckskin is best washed by hand in cold to warm (not hot!) water with Woolite or soft soaps such as the brown bars of Fels Naptha. I grate up about a quarter bar to wash my shirt (it's usually very dirty by the time I get around to washing it). Let the buckskin soak awhile before you add soap and actually work it. Frequently I change the water after the initial soapless soaking. Soap can be rubbed directly on really dirty spots (and pits!). The first washing of a garment can be a bit traumatic (fear of the unknown), but soon becomes common course. Some people are stubborn though. At this writing,   my friend and neighbor hasn't washed his shirt yet--and he made it four years ago!

After thoroughly washing and rinsing an article (hopefully until the water squeezes out clean), I go ahead and wring it out by hand, then stretch and pull it back out to its original shape. I then blot it, roll it up in some dry towels to further remove excess moisture, often letting it sit for a few hours. When unrolled, it is about the consistency of a slightly damp washcloth. I then just drape it somewhere over something smooth (like a hide frame), preferably outside where the fresh air can circulate around it. It is best not to hang a shirt on a clotheshanger because the corners of the hanger may "poof out" the shoulders of the shirt. If it dries this way, those buldges will be hard to eliminate unless you rewet them. As one side of the garment dries, I often turn it inside out.

When the article is still slightly damp, I prefer to briefly shake, rub and pull it briskly all over. This loosens everything up and allows deep-seated moisture to evaporate quicker. I then put the garment on so as it further dries it readjusts to my body shape and movements. You can let a garment dry thoroughly before you resoften it if you want--it just takes a little more work. Fringe especially tends to stiffen and must be vigorously rubbed. This resoftening after washing is nowhere near the job that working the skin soft and dry in the frame was.

Avoid electric washers and driers unless you can carefully control the temperatures and lengths of the cycles. I have, via unintentional experimentation, had bad luck with both. A standard washing action and cycle is too rough and too long; it's especially hard on laced seams. The "warm" water setting on a washer can be too hot for buckskin. Any prolonged heat in a drier tends to "pinch and shrivel" the buckskin fibers (just as with wool) and you may suddenly find your shirt with a new surface texture and a new, smaller size! The tumbling action of a drier is handy for making a garment very supple if you can set the machine to blow only cold (or very slightly warm) air.

After extended wear and repeated washings, buckskin clothing will gradually lose its smoked color and return to an off-white shade. Usually by this stage the fibers are well conditioned and softened and the garment will, if anything, become softer after each washing. The smoke is obviously beneficial to the skin, however, and if you desire, you can resmoke your garments, following the same procedures you did initially. Resmoking is handy when you want to match up an outfit, say an old shirt with a freshly made pair of pants.

CONCLUDING COMMENTS

With the conclusion of this booklet, some "wrapping up" thoughts come to mind. Most of the suggestions, dos and don'ts, explanations and hints I make are the results of my own experiences. I have emphasized ways of proceed-through the buckskin process and subsequent clothing manufacture with which I am familiar and have found successful. My purpose has been to make these endeavors easier for you, to provide enough background information, reasons and examples so you won't have to experience as much trial and error, "traveling blind" as I did.

A major reality remains, however. When I did my first buckskin, I didn't know ninety five per cent of what comprises this booklet--and my first buckskin turned out okay (not perfect, not bad, but above average). It remains as the front panel on my everyday shirt.

So, I shall repeat my basic premise for successful buckskinning, as each person's situation will be unique: Learn what you <u>must</u> <u>do</u> to a hide to turn it into buckskin, what you must accomplish in each step of the process, by whatever means are available to you. In the process, you will learn alot more--what you can do (options, variations), what you can "get away with," and what you <u>must</u> <u>not</u> do! And, no matter what you do, it will be a learning process.

I wish you success!

Jim Riggs

119

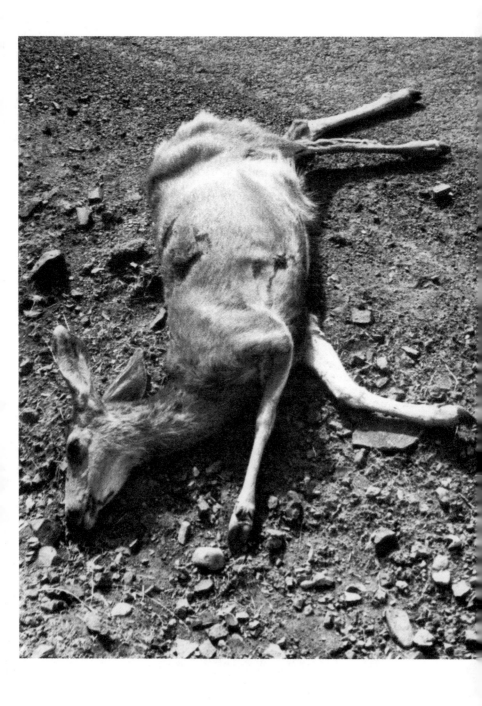

A DEER IS MORE THAN VENISON ON THE TABLE

Each year as the hunting seasons for antelope, big-horn sheep, deer and elk come along, I am reminded of the contrast between the orientation of the modern hunter and his aboriginal counterpart. While the desire to bring home fresh, wild meat remains basic to the hunting incentive, the means, and the hunter's understanding of the natural environment and the game he seeks, seem to have changed considerably.

A modern hunting excursion into the outdoors is a welcome and enjoyable respite from the workaday world, but too often the technological, recreational and "convenience" aspects (four-wheel drives, campers, portable televisions, high-powered scopes and rifles, ad infinitum) subtly retard the progress and intensity of the natural experience. Most peoples' everyday lives are so far removed from the natural cycles of life that hunting trips take them into alien environments. Their experience there seldom lasts long enough for the alienation to grow into familiarity and understanding.

I think it is man's desire, perhaps unrealized need, that drives him to the hunt, but his lack of knowledge and commitment ultimately lessen that experience and lock him into his alien role. This opinion is reaffirmed whenever I come across a dead deer, one that was shot but evidently ran aways before falling, and I must conclude that the hunter had not the patience, skill nor responsibility to track the animal to its final resting place. In rugged country it is not unusual to find an elk carcass with only the hindquarters and backstraps taken...too much hassle to return for a second or third load, I guess.

When I acquire deer hides from hunters and flesh them in preparation for making buckskin, I am continually amazed at the large sheets and hunks of once-superb meat they've left adhering to the skins. Most hides I process are improperly skinned and have two to five or more pounds of meat still attached. It's absurd! The modern way seems to be one of carelessly slashing the skin off sheerly for the thrill of wielding a new knife. A skin is more efficiently and nearly as expediently removed by "fisting" it off--that is, by separating the connective tissue between skin and carcass by hand, after making only a few initial incisions with a knife.

Perhaps the worst of these situations involve a minority of those who hunt, but they occur frequently and do

not speak well for the health and evolution of a modern
hunting ethic. In these situations it is not so much
the waste of meat that bothers me, for the carrion-eat-
ers--the coyotes, vultures, skunks, beetles, yellowjac-
kets and the like--will devour most of the carcasses.
What they leave will gradually return to the soil as
part of the organic process. What leaves me scratching
my head in wonder is man's attitude and his uncompleted
responsibility to the natural cycles of life.

The hunting of big game in aboriginal times and
hunting today by those who live closely with nature or
have at least once experienced that lifeway, presents
quite a different picture. Hunting was not recreation
or sport, but a necessary and integral component of existence. It is logical to assume that the challenge of
the hunt was enjoyed, that the continual application and
testing of one's cumulative knowledge and skills was
stimulating, but the reasons for hunting were deeply
rooted in sincere need for the animal's meat, hide and
additional byproducts. Hunting was directly a life-
supporting activity.

While hunting supplied the aboriginal diet with pro-
tein and nutrition not steadily obtainable from other
food sources, it is interesting to note that in none of
the Pacific Northwestern native cultures was hunting the
dominant food-providing economic activity. On the coast,
fishing and shellfish gathering dominated. Along the
Columbia River and its tributaries draining the plateau
regions of Washington, Oregon and Idaho, salmon and roots
comprised the food staples. In the arid Great Basin between the Sierras and Rockies, about two thirds of the
diet was comprised of vegetable foods, mostly seeds.
Whole technologies and implements were developed for the
harvesting and processing of seeds, some individually
smaller than a pinhead, but lucrative because they could
be collected in great quantities. West of the Cascades,
economic activities were about equally represented by
plant gathering, fishing and hunting.

The importance of specific big game animals varied
greatly from one region and culture to another. The Es-
kimo hunted mainly sea mammals, natives of the tundra
and boreal forest the caribou, Great Plains horsemen the
bison. In the Great Basin, due to the paucity of larger
game, the jackrabbit dominated. But the deer was in-
digenous to nearly all of North America and is still the
most frequently and consistently hunted big game. It is
the aboriginal's conception of the deer that sets him a-
part from the modern hunter.

Because the deer was the source of so many important
materials to native cultures, each hunter well under-
stood his prey; he killed the deer, but he appreciated

all that it gave him. Before the hunt he often fasted
and took a sweatbath to cleanse his mind and body, to
pray for success and to properly attune his attitude
and energies. He thanked the deer and the Great Spirit
for helping to fulfill his needs. These were not cursory utterances or affectations--"corny" by modern at-
titudes--these were genuinely expressed feelings from
people who had grown their entire lives knowing and de-
pending on nature intimately enough to realize that nothing should be taken for granted, that mental attitudes
do influence seemingly secular cause-effect relation-
ships. To teach respect, humility and generosity, in
many native cultures it was customary for a boy not to
partake of his first deer, but to distribute it among
his family, relatives and friends.

Aboriginal cultures, though all materially based on
available natural resources, varied considerably due to
differing origins and adaptations to widely differing
environments. All of these peoples obviously did not
utilize all parts of all deer killed, but their knowledge of how they could, when needed, make use of nearly
the entire animal is truly amazing. I believe that most
modern hunters are further separated from their natural
environment and their prey because they lack the familiarity that grows from, and is based on, this "need to
use" concept. The uses for a deer described here have
been collected from many sources and it is unlikely that
any single aboriginal group was familiar with them all.
Most uses apply to other hoofed big game as well as the
deer.

Aboriginal hunters may have procured deer with bow
and arrow, the atlatl (spearthrower) and dart, tough rawhide or plant fiber snares, via pitfall traps, coordi-
nated drives into enclosures or over cliffs or numerous
other methods. A freshly killed deer was first eviscer-
ated, then cleanly skinned.

Sometimes the head skin was removed whole, stuffed
with dry leaves or grasses so it would hold its natural
shape as it dried, and later used as a hunting decoy.
Other times the head skin was left attached so the whole
skin could be draped over a hunter with the stuffed deer
head resting on top of the hunter's own head for use as
effective camouflage in stalking more game. These decoy
methods were extremely effective, but a hunter would be
taking his life rather lightly if he tried this in the
ballyhoo of a modern hunting season!

In the Great Basin where large game was at a premi-
um, the people developed some ingenious uses for normally marginal parts of the skin. "Hock" moccasins were
made from the skin encompassing the heel area--about mid-
leg--of each of the deer's hind legs. These tubular sec-

tions of skin were girdled above and below the hocks, then peeled off like socks; they were naturally shaped to fit small human feet. Modification consisted only of sewing closed the lower end of the skin tube to form the toe portion of each moccasin and adding a couple skin ties to the upper part so it could be bound around the wearer's ankle. The skin was seldom tanned for these quickly constructed moccasins, and they were often finished inside out, hair side against the wearer's foot for added warmth. In the Canadian north, mukluks from moose hocks are still occasionally made this same way.

Another "quickie" moccasin, termed the Fremont style for the early culture in Utah where it was first found and described, used all four lower leg skins from a deer or bighorn sheep. These untanned pieces of skin were cleverly cut and sewed together so that the dewclaws attached to the skins served as hobnails or grips, four on the sole of each moccasin. One animal's leg skins yielded one pair of moccasins. Nowadays the lower legs are cut from the carcass and discarded, but an enterprising native could make a pair of hock or Fremont moccasins and still have the rest of the hide to tan for clothing.

The fresh hide was either tanned immediately or stretched out and dried. It could then be kept indefinitely for later tanning or used untanned. Untanned skins with the hair left on were used for mats and bedding. Eventually, these became fairly soft from use, and by the time most of the hair had broken or worn off, they were made into moccasins or other articles of rawhide, or tanned as buckskin.

Rawhide was prepared and used with varying degrees of refinement. Most simply a skin was soaked in water or buried in the ground for a few days until the hair slipped off easily. Strips cut from a hide prepared in this way were especially useful for sturdily binding things together, because rawhide stretches when wet and shrinks tightly while drying. Larger pieces were used for drum heads. For moccasin soles, quivers, knife and bow sheaths, saddlebags and storage containers, rawhide was further processed. The hair and epidermal layer of skin were scraped from a stretched, dried hide which was then thoroughly and systematically pounded with round stones to make it thicker and more pliable. Most often, hides heavier than deer were prepared in this way.

Deer hides were usually made into buckskin. The hair and epidermal layer were removed by either wet or dry scraping and the tough, tightly adhering connective tissue scraped from the flesh side of a skin. The hide was then soaked for a few minutes up to a day in an emulsion of the deer's brain mixed with water. Sometimes the

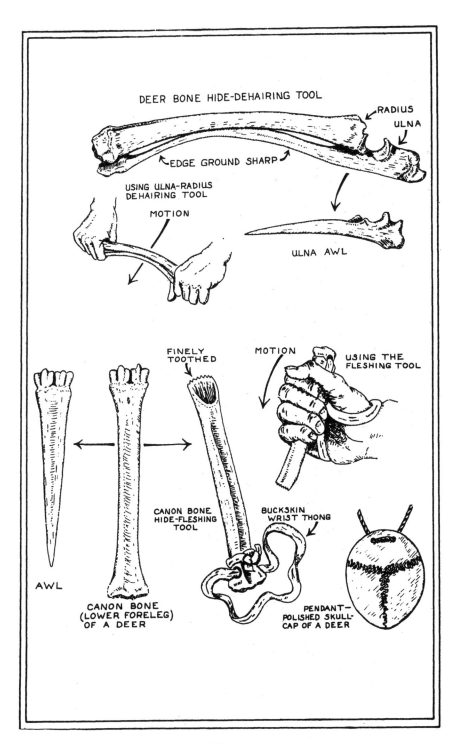

DEER BONE HIDE-DEHAIRING TOOL

RADIUS
ULNA

EDGE GROUND SHARP

USING ULNA-RADIUS
DEHAIRING TOOL

MOTION

ULNA AWL

FINELY
TOOTHED

MOTION

USING THE
FLESHING TOOL

CANON BONE
HIDE-FLESHING
TOOL

BUCKSKIN
WRIST THONG

AWL

CANON BONE
(LOWER FORELEG)
OF A DEER

PENDANT—
POLISHED SKULL-
CAP OF A DEER

brain was mashed and beaten into a paste which was rubbed into the skin. After braining, the skin was wrung
out to eliminate all excess moisture, then worked continually by hand or laced into a square pole frame and
worked with oar-shaped sticks until thoroughly dry, soft
and pure white. Lastly, if intended for everyday wear
and use, the white buckskin was sewed into a bag shape
and suspended over a smudge fire, first one side, then
the other, until it turned the desired shade of yellow,
tan or brown. The color depended on the length of time
it was smoked and the type of vegetation used to create
the smoke. Smoking helped preserve the skin, gave it a
pleasing aroma and allowed it to dry soft after getting
wet or being washed.

This basic process, with many variations from one
culture to another, produced what we call Indian tan or
smoke and brain tan buckskin--the soft, warm, strong and
durable material many tribes used for their clothing,
decorative bags, cradleboard coverings, etc., almost
anything we use cloth or leather for these days.

If the brains were not to be used immediately for
tanning, they were lightly boiled and spread to dry in
the sun, mixed with dried moss and further dried or
sealed in a length of intestine so they would keep until
needed. They also could be eaten.

Deer skins with the hair left on could be tanned soft
for robes and blankets, but these were hardly worth the
hard work of tanning because deer hair, unlike that of
furbearing animals, is hollow and brittle and continually
breaks and sheds.

The deer's tail was either left on the skin or removed and used for a decoration. The ears could be carefully skinned out, inflated like a balloon and dried in
that shape, then, with the insertion of a few pebbles or
tiny foot bones from the deer, re-bound closed around a
stick handle and used for a ceremonial rattle. From a
buck the scrotal skin was softened and fashioned into a
naturally shaped small utility pouch.

The whole feet, hooves included, could be coarsely
chopped up and boiled to extract the valuable oil which
rose to the surface of the water and could be scooped off
with a small container. One deer's feet yield only a-
bout a tablespoonful of oil, so this process was usually
done only when many feet could be boiled together. This
neatsfoot-like oil is an excellent dressing for skins--
it was sometimes added to the brain emulsion for tanning
buckskins--and was used to condition and preserve antler,
bone and wooden tools.

Even the deer's eyes had a special use. The fluid
inside them was a medium for mixing with powdered earth
pigments such as red ochre to make paint.

Before a skinned deer was cut up, the hunter removed the all-important sinew. Sinew is a term for the
tendons. Leg tendons are rounded in cross section, en-
cased in a tough outer covering and must be pounded with
smooth stones or soaked and split open to expose the
soft, tough inner fibers. The Achilles tendon in your
own heel is a good example of this type of sinew.

Other sinew from the shoulder, back and rump shows
as thin, shiny sheets on the surface of the meat. The
longest sinew in a deer extends in two flat sheets, each
about two inches wide, from the shoulderblades to the
pelvis along each side of the backbone. For removal, it
must be severed at each end where it narrows and peeled
from the backstrap (tenderloin) meat to which it ad-
heres. A fingernail easily separates this naturally
striated flat sinew into thin fibers. Sinews were
scraped clean and dried for later use.

In aboriginal times, finely shredded sinew fibers
served as strong sewing thread, binding material for
stone points and feathers on arrows and any other bindings calling for something finer than rawhide. Sinew
was the strongest natural material available for twisting into bow strings and snares, and bundles or strips
of shredded sinew were affixed to the backs of wooden
bows with glue made of boiled fish skin, boiled deer or
other mammal skin. Sinew-backed bows were not more power-
ful, but were more elastic and kept the wood from shat-
tering. Like rawhide, sinew fibers were moistened, usually in the mouth, before application, and they shrank
and tightened as they dried.

The meat provided by the deer was the main reason
the animal was sought, and could be prepared in many
ways. Usually the heart, liver, tongue and occasionally
lungs and kidneys were eaten first as they were not easily preserved. Some portions of meat were eaten raw, or
simply thrust onto sticks and roasted over the fire. As
the longbones were picked clean of meat, they were
cracked open with stones and the nutritious marrow sucked
out.

Boiled meat was a favorite. Lacking containers that
could be placed directly over a fire, the Northwest cultures developed other ways for boiling foods. Many fist-
size or smaller, rounded stones were gathered and placed
in a fire until they became red-hot. Then, with wooden
tongs, they were dropped into watertight wooden boxes,
carved wooden or stone bowls or tightly woven baskets
with the meat and water. More hot stones were added,
stirred and the cooled ones removed until the water had
boiled the meat the desired length of time.

Although men on a hunt lacked these kinds of containers so common around the permanent camps, they still in-

vented ways to boil meat. Sometimes they propped the ribcage open, filled it with as much water and meat as it would hold, and proceeded with the same stone-boiling process. Another method was to scoop out a bowl-shaped depression in the ground and line it with a portion of the hide or the opened stomach to serve as the boiling container. Sometimes the boiling was accomplished in the opened stomach draped bag-like from three or four upright sticks set into the ground. The contents of the stomach were often boiled along with the added meat and then the stomach itself, now thoroughly cooked, was also eaten--a perhaps not so tidy feast which, nevertheless, left no dirty dishes!

To preserve meat, make it lightweight and easy to carry, it was sliced into thin sheets or long strips and dried in the sun or hung on quickly constructed pole racks over a smudgy fire of good-tasting wood and smoked for a couple days. Even after smoking or sun drying for a couple hours, the surface of the meat glazed over and it became easier to handle and transport than when fresh. This drying, of course, produced the original jerky.

Pemmican was made by pounding dried meat to a fine powder and mixing it about half and half by weight with rendered fat. This mixture was packed into rawhide bags or lengths of cleaned intestine where it would keep indefinitely. Because pemmican was so concentrated, compact and supplied the native with almost all the nutrients his body needed, except for Vitamin C, it was and still is the most perfect food to carry on long journeys. When available, dried and pounded serviceberries or other fruits were added to the pemmican to provide the Vitamin C.

Intestines were very utilitarian. They could be sliced open, scraped clean, washed, cooked and eaten. Tubular sections were turned inside out, cleaned and, with the ends tied closed, used to store rendered fat, boiled brains, pemmican and even to carry water. They were sometimes taken through the same process as buckskin--scraping, braining, softening and smoking--and then cut into long strips for strong cordage.

Because the deer's bladder is conveniently shaped and naturally waterproof, it was fashioned into a small pouch specifically intended to carry materials that must stay dry, especially tinder for firestarting and the punky wooden bits for the hand-twirled fire drill.

Some Northern Paiute people of the Great Basin made interesting use of the deer's spleen. As a poison for tipping arrows intended mostly for warfare, it supposedly took immediate effect, produced swelling and eventually death, but if used on game did not affect the edibility of the meat. An old Paiute man from Surprise Valley describes the process:

"Our poison is made from the deer's akwatsi, black looking stuff on the intestine which looks like the liver but is smaller. Cook it in the ashes and let it dry. It smells bad. Stick the arrowpoint in and let it dry, or rub on the poison with the finger. There is no cure, so you have to be careful, especially if your finger is cut." (It is probable that there is nothing inherently poisonous in the spleen, but that blood poisoning could easily stem from an arrow wound becoming infected. Other Paiute poisoning methods call for enticing a rattlesnake to bite a fresh liver or spleen, letting these ferment for a few days, then sticking the arrowpoints in the rotted meat.)

Several years ago, determined to make full use of a deer, I cooked up the spleen thinking it was part of the liver. My "spleen stew" tasted absolutely horrible, but I dutifully ate most of it, all the while telling myself only my own food prejudices made it taste so bad. I suffered no ill effects other than revulsion! Most unpleasant experiences tend to mellow with time in one's memory, but that stewed spleen just gets worse every time I think about it.

Bone and antler probably provided more raw materials for manufactures than any other parts of the deer. They can be used similarly for many tools, but antler was better suited for some. It is softer, more elastic and resilient than bone and has less tendency to crack and split.

Antler tines were first girdled with a sharp stone, then snapped into convenient lengths for use as pressure flakers in the manufacture of chipped stone scrapers, knives, drills and projectile points. Heavier sections of antler were used as billets for percussion stoneworking.

Along the coast, antler was cut and ground into wedges for splitting wood. Large antler tines functioned as crosspiece handles on hardwood rootdigging sticks. Each tine had an inch-wide hole drilled laterally through its center so it could be slipped onto the top end of the digger to provide better leverage when the pointed stick was shoved into the ground next to a fat, juicy root. Sometimes the antler tines themselves were used to dig roots.

Sections of antler were commonly shaped into knife, scraper and other handles, delicately incised and carved beads, figurines, decorative pendants, plus most of the uses made of bone as listed below. During the rutting season as an aid to hunting, whole antlers were clacked together by a concealed hunter to attract other deer.

Deer bones come in such a variety of dimensions that

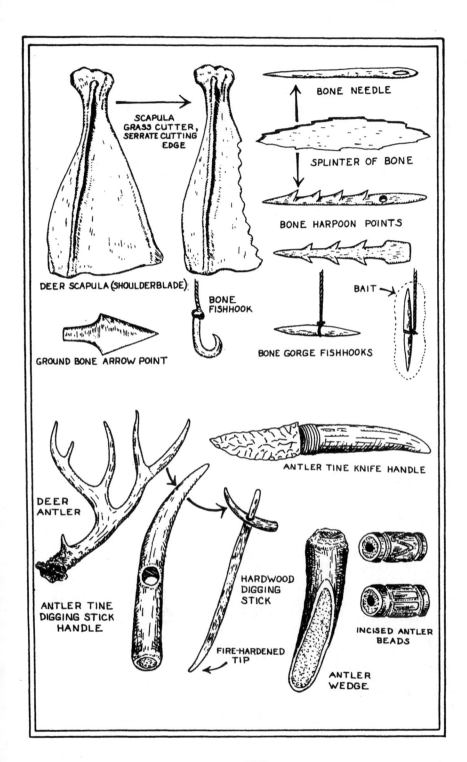

SCAPULA GRASS CUTTER, SERRATE CUTTING EDGE

BONE NEEDLE

SPLINTER OF BONE

BONE HARPOON POINTS

DEER SCAPULA (SHOULDERBLADE)

BONE FISHHOOK

BAIT

GROUND BONE ARROW POINT

BONE GORGE FISHHOOKS

ANTLER TINE KNIFE HANDLE

DEER ANTLER

HARDWOOD DIGGING STICK

INCISED ANTLER BEADS

ANTLER TINE DIGGING STICK HANDLE

FIRE-HARDENED TIP

ANTLER WEDGE

many tools and articles are already suggested by the
natural forms, whether it be an unmodified longbone used
as a fish-killing club or the tiny, smooth splinter-like
bones from a deer's front feet that serve as as preformed
needles with only the drilling of eyes. With some incis-
ing here, some grinding there, some sanding and polishing,
aboriginal man produced awls for basketry and skin working, pipes, beads of all sizes, ceremonial and game calling whistles, combs, points for arrows, spears and har-
poons, drill bits, net gauges, weaving shuttles, mat
creasers, simple to elaborate carved effigies, even snow
goggles. The splinters of bone that remained after the
marrow was extracted were shaped into needles, pins, dice
and other gaming pieces, small awls and many kinds of
fishhooks.
    Certain bones lended themselves to specialized tools.
The thin, flat scapula or shoulderblade was cut or broken
to a jagged edge along one side and used to cut bunches
of grasses for basketry, seed extraction, matting and
thatching materials. Sometimes the deer's jawbone was
similarly used, the teeth functioning as the cutting
edge.
    One end of the canon bone, the lowest longbone in a
deer's front leg, was cut on a bevel and tiny, sharp
teeth were notched along the beveled edge. With a buckskin loop attached to the other end to brace the tanner's
wrist, this tool was used with a downward stroking motion
to remove any flesh, fat or connective tissue remaining
on a hide.
    The combination ulna and radius bones, also from the
deer's foreleg, were used for the next step in tanning
by the wet-scrape method. The long, thin edge of the
ulna was ground sharp with abrasive stones and the naturally attached radius served as the handgrip. After the
hide had been soaked in water long enough to slip the
hair and loosen the epidermis, it was draped over a
smooth section of log and the ulna-radius tool was used
like a drawknife to scrape off the unwanted material.
Except for human skill and labor, the deer supplied all
the necessary materials for tanning its own hide!
    The myriad artifacts of deer and other bone produced
in aboriginal cultures were defined by the tasks that
needed to be accomplished and limited only by the imagination of the aboriginal mind. Archaeologists (perhaps
limited, somewhat ironically, by their own imaginations)
have excavated many obviously specialized bone and antler
implements whose function in the native cultures still
remains a mystery. I have barely touched on the known
tools and their uses here.
    Somewhere back in time--or perhaps ahead in time--on
a crisp morning in the Moon of Plenty Harvest, a buckskin-

clad figure crouches patiently in a chokecherry thicket above a well-used deer trail. The wind is right. His sinew-backed yew-wood bow is well greased with deer fat and curved taut by its tightly twisted deer sinew string. The arrow of oceanspray wood held lightly in his fingers is tipped with a black obsidian point he deftly flaked with the tip of a deer's antler and carefully bound to the shaft, like the three hawk feathers at the other end, with thread-thin sinew fibers first moistened in his mouth.

He has used the strength of the deer to fashion his tools so he may procure more deer. Through his ability to learn, the strength of the deer has become his own strength. It is alive inside him. He waits quietly while an unconcerned junco examines shriveled chokecherries among the branches above him. The deer will come; it always has.

Man has always been a hunter, a predator. As with all predators, the act of killing has been a necessary and integral part of living. But I believe there are moral and immoral approaches to killing. I believe any modern hunter can learn much from the beliefs and practices of the aboriginal man who lived closely with the earth. And perhaps he might find it rewarding to experiment with some of the aboriginal uses of the deer.

Peeling backstrap sinew from a deer carcass

132

"...if I'd a knowed what a trouble it was to make a book I wouldn't a tackled it and I ain't agoing to no more."

I think Mark Twain said that.

"Ah elk urine--a book ain't no way to show somebody if'n they got all the grain and membrane off'n their hide--you gotta just stand there and point it out to 'em while they're aworkin' on it, and sometimes even then you can't really tell..."

I said that.

Recommended Tools and Resources

Ordering information for tools that will help you succeed.

Dry-scraper $87

The key tool for dry-scrape brain-tanning

Some tanning tasks are easily done with home-made and improvised tools. Dry scraping, however, is very dependent on the quality of the tool. Your tool should hold an extremely sharp edge and be comfortable to use. Master tanner and tool smith Darry Wood designed this tool, and they are without a doubt the best we've ever laid our hands on. The high quality steel blades hold that super keen edge you need for pleasurable, efficient scraping. The 115 degree angle prevents 'chattering' and the full 2.5 lb weight helps this tool do a lot of the work for you.

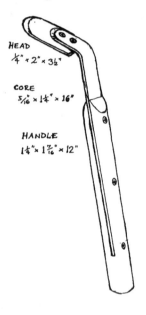

HEAD
¼" × 2" × 3½"

CORE
5/16 × 1¼" × 16"

HANDLE
1¼" × 1 7/16" × 12"

Specs: The blade is oil-quenched tool steel tempered to a Rockwell hardness of c-58. The blade is joined (using 1/4" fine-threaded machine bolts) to a 5/16" thick cold finish steel core, which in turn is set in a hardwood handle and fixed with slotted brass screws. The handle stock is oak, alder or Douglas fir.

"I got several of these scrapers years ago and they are indeed the best I've ever used." **Jim Riggs**

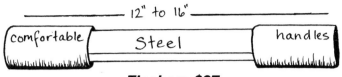

Fleshers $27

made from mill-planer blades

Mill-planer blades make great fleshing (and wet-scraping) tools because they are made of an extremely high quality steel that holds its edge like nothing else. Once properly dulled (which we do for you), you won't need to mess with the edge for the next 100 hides (which probably means your lifetime). These blades are recycled from logging mills and come with simple rubber handles.

Softening Cable $8

A favorite hand softening tool, these are 3/16 inch diameter, five feet long and come with cable clamps. One cable lasts a very long time.

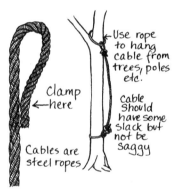

Pumice $5

Pumice is a volcanic rock that works like natural sandpaper. It'll give your hides a noticeably softer surface texture and speedily remove unwanted membrane and blemishes.

These rocks are hand-selected for us from the sides of Mt Shasta. They are nicely rounded and very comfortable to hold and use. One rock will last you at least 50 hides.

Blue Mtn Buckskin
$19.95

You can order more copies of *Blue Mountain Buckskin* from your favorite dealer, or directly from Traditional Tanners (see next page).

Deerskins into Buckskins

by Matt Richards

- Book $19.95
- Video $25.00

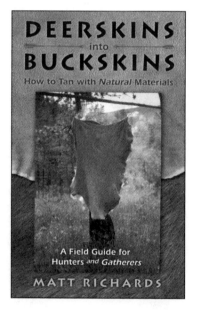

This is the best-selling guide to the other method of brain tanning known as 'wet-scraping'. Matt Richards guides you step by step from raw skin to velvety soft buckskin. The book is 160 pages and includes over 130 photos and illustrations. The video is 2 hrs long and shows you visually each step of the process. You can learn from either the book or the video, but they work best together.